Workshop on Computational Models of Language Acquisition and Loss 2012

Held at the 13th Conference of the European Chapter of the Association for Computational Linguistics (EACL 2012)

Avignon, France
23 – 27 April 2012

ISBN: 978-1-62276-492-1

Printed from e-media with permission by:

Curran Associates, Inc.
57 Morehouse Lane
Red Hook, NY 12571

Some format issues inherent in the e-media version may also appear in this print version.

Printed by Curran Associates, Inc. (2012)

For permission requests, please contact the Association for Computational Linguistics at the address below.

Association for Computational Linguistics
209 N. Eighth Street
Stroudsburg, Pennsylvania 18360

Phone: 1-570-476-8006
Fax: 1-570-476-0860

acl@aclweb.org

Additional copies of this publication are available from:

Curran Associates, Inc.
57 Morehouse Lane
Red Hook, NY 12571 USA
Phone: 845-758-0400
Fax: 845-758-2634
Email: curran@proceedings.com
Web: www.proceedings.com

Introduction

The past decades have seen a massive expansion in the application of statistical and machine learning methods to speech and natural language processing. This work has yielded impressive results which have generally been viewed as engineering achievements. Recently researchers have begun to investigate the relevance of computational learning methods for research on human language acquisition and loss.

The human ability to acquire and process language has long attracted interest and generated much debate due to the apparent ease with which such a complex and dynamic system is learnt and used on the face of ambiguity, noise and uncertainty. On the other hand, changes in language abilities during aging and eventual losses related to conditions such as Alzheimer's disease and dementia have also attracted considerable investigative efforts. Parallels between the acquisition and loss have been raised, and a better understanding of the mechanisms involved in both, and of how the algorithms used to access concepts are affected in pathological cases can lead to earlier diagnosis and more targeted treatments.

The use of computational modeling is a relatively recent trend boosted by advances in machine learning techniques, and the availability of resources like corpora of child and child-directed sentences, and data from psycholinguistic tasks by normal and pathological groups. Many of the existing computational models attempt to study language tasks under cognitively plausible criteria (such as memory and processing limitations that humans face), and to explain the developmental stages observed in the acquisition and evolution of the language abilities.

This was the third edition of this workshop that was first held at ACL 2007 in Prague and then in EACL 2009 in Athens. The workshop was targeted at anyone interested in the relevance of computational techniques for understanding first, second and bilingual language acquisition and change or loss in normal and pathological conditions. We invited submissions on relevant topics, including:

- Computational learning theory and analysis of language learning
- Computational models of first, second and bilingual language acquisition or of the evolution of language
- Computational models and analysis of factors that influence language acquisition and loss in different age groups and cultures
- Data resources and tools for investigating computational models of human language processes
- Empirical and theoretical comparisons of the environment and its impact on acquisition
- Investigations and comparisons of supervised, unsupervised and weakly-supervised methods for learning

Submissions included works on specific languages like English, Portuguese and Hebrew, and also crosslinguistic studies. Besides paper presentations the technical program included resources and systems demonstrations, and two invited talks by Mark Steedman, from University of Edinburgh (UK) and Alessandro Lenci, from University of Pisa (Italy).

1 Acknowledgments

We would like to thank the support of CNPq and CAPES-COFECUB (Projects 551964/2011-1, 478222/2011-4, 202007/2010-3 and 707/11) and of the labex (laboratoire d'excellence) Empirical Foundation of Linguistics.

Organizers:

Robert Berwick, Massachusetts Institute of Technology (USA)
Anna Korhonen, University of Cambridge (UK)
Thierry Poibeau, LaTTiCe-CNRS (France) and University of Cambridge (UK)
Aline Villavicencio, Federal University of Rio Grande do Sul (Brazil) and Massachussets Institute of Technology (USA)

Program Committee:

Afra Alishahi, Tilburg University (Netherlands)
Colin J Bannard, University of Texas at Austin (USA)
Marco Baroni, University of Trento (Italy)
Jim Blevins, University of Cambridge (UK)
Rens Bod, University of Amsterdam (Netherlands)
Antal van den Bosch, Tilburg University (Netherlands)
Alexander Clark, Royal Holloway, University of London (UK)
Robin Clark, University of Pennsylvania (USA)
Matthew W. Crocker, Saarland University (Germany)
James Cussens, University of York (UK)
Walter Daelemans, University of Antwerp (Belgium) and Tilburg University (Netherlands)
Barry Devereux, University of Cambridge (UK)
Sonja Eisenbeiss, University of Essex (UK)
Afsaneh Fazly, University of Toronto (Canada)
Cynthia Fisher, University of Illinois (USA)
Jeroen Geertzen, University of Cambridge (UK)
Henriette Hendriks, University of Cambridge (UK)
Marco Idiart, Federal University of Rio Grande do Sul (Brazil)
Aravind Joshi, University of Pennsylvania (USA)
Shalom Lappin, King's College London (UK)
Alessandro Lenci, University of Pisa (Italy)
Igor Malioutov, Massachusetts Institute of Technology (USA)
Marie-Catherine de Marneffe, Stanford University (USA)
Fanny Meunier, Lumière Lyon 2 University (France)
Brian Murphy, Carnegie Mellon University (USA)
Maria Alice Parente, Federal University of Rio Grande do Sul (Brazil)
Massimo Poesio, University of Essex (UK)
Brechtje Post, University of Cambridge (UK)
Ari Rappoport, The Hebrew University of Jerusalem (Israel)
Dan Roth, University of Illinois at Urbana-Champaign (USA)
Kenji Sagae, University of Southern California (USA)
Sabine Schulte im Walde, University of Stuttgart (Germany)
Ekaterina Shutova, University of Cambridge (UK)
Maity Siqueira, Federal University of Rio Grande do Sul (Brazil)
Mark Steedman, University of Edinburgh (UK)

Shuly Wintner, University of Haifa (Israel)
Charles Yang, University of Pennsylvania (USA)
Beracah Yankama, Massachusetts Institute of Technology (USA)
Menno van Zaanen, Tilburg University (Netherlands)
Michael Zock, LIF, CNRS, Marseille (France)

Invited Speakers:

Mark Steedman, University of Edinburgh (UK) and
Alessandro Lenci, University of Pisa (Italy)

Table of Contents

Conference Program

Tuesday, April 24, 2012

8:55 Opening Session

(9:00) Session 1:Language Evolution and Learning

9:00 *Distinguishing Contact-Induced Change from Language Drift in Genetically Related Languages*
T. Mark Ellison and Luisa Miceli

9:30 *Empiricist Solutions to Nativist Puzzles by means of Unsupervised TSG*
Rens Bod and Margaux Smets

10:00 Coffee Break

(10:30) Invited Talk I - Mark Steedman (University of Edinburgh, UK)

Probabilistic Models of Grammar Acquisition
Mark Steedman

(11:30) Session 2:Demonstrations

A Morphologically Annotated Hebrew CHILDES Corpus
Aviad Albert, Brian MacWhinney, Bracha Nir and Shuly Wintner

An annotated English child language database
Aline Villavicencio, Beracah Yankama, Rodrigo Wilkens, Marco Idiart and Robert Berwick

Searching the Annotated Portuguese Childes Corpora
Rodrigo Wilkens

Webservices for Bayesian Learning
Muntsa Padró and Núria Bel

12:30 Lunch Break

Tuesday, April 24, 2012 (continued)

(14:00) Invited Talk II - Alessandro Lenci (University of Pisa, Italy)

Unseen features. Collecting semantic data from congenital blind subjects
Alessandro Lenci, Marco Baroni and Giovanna Marotta

(15:00) Session 3: Phonology and Syntax I

15:00 *PHACTS about activation-based word similarity effects*
Basilio Calderone and Chiara Celata

15:15 *I say have you say tem: profiling verbs in children data in English and Portuguese*
Rodrigo Wilkens and Aline Villavicencio

15:30 Coffee Break

(16:00) Session 4: Phonology and Syntax II

16:00 *Get out but don't fall down: verb-particle constructions in child language*
Aline Villavicencio, Marco Idiart, Carlos Ramisch, Vítor Araújo, Beracah Yankama and Robert Berwick

16:30 *Phonologic Patterns of Brazilian Portuguese: a grapheme to phoneme converter based study*
Vera Vasilévski

17:00 Closing Remarks

Distinguishing Contact-Induced Change from Language Drift in Genetically Related Languages

T. Mark Ellison
Psychology
University of Western Australia
Mark.Ellison@uwa.edu.au

Luisa Miceli
Linguistics
University of Western Australia
lmiceli@cyllene.uwa.edu.au

Abstract

Languages evolve, undergoing repeated small changes, some with permanent effect and some not. Changes affecting a language may be independent or contact-induced. Independent changes arise internally or, if externally, from non-linguistic causes. En masse, such changes cause isolated languages to drift apart in lexical form and grammatical structure. Contact-induced changes can happen when languages share speakers, or when their speakers are in contact.

Frequently, languages in contact are related, having a common ancestor from which they still retain visible structure. This relatedness makes it difficult to distinguish contact-induced change from inherited similarities.

In this paper, we present a simulation of contact-induced change. We show that it is possible to distinguish contact-induced change from independent change given (a) enough data, and (b) that the contact-induced change is strong enough. For a particular model, we determine how much data is enough to distinguish these two cases at $p < 0.05$.

1 Introduction

Evolutionary change happens when structures are copied, the copying is inexact, and the survival of copies is uncertain. Many structures undergo this kind of reproduction, change and death: biological organisms, fashions, languages. Often evolutionary change leaves little or no trace, except for those copies which are present at the moment. In these cases, determining the evolutionary history of a family of structures involves comparing surviving copies and making inferences from where they correspond and where they differ.

Language is, for the most part, one of those cases. Most languages have not had a writing system until recently, and so their history has left no direct trace. Since the 18th century, linguists have been comparing languages to reconstruct both common parents and individual histories for these languages (Jones, 1786; Schleicher, 1861; Brugmann, 1884, for example).

In this paper, we hope to contribute to this effort by presenting a formal model of a particular kind of evolutionary change, namely **contact-induced change**, and placing limits on when its past presence can be inferred from synchronic evidence.

Contact-induced change can happen when speakers of different languages come in contact, or where there is a sizeable group of bi- or multilinguals. We distinguish two different types. One type, **contact-induced assimilation** (CIA) changes languages so that they become more similar to each other. This is the type of contact-induced change that is most obvious and that has been best studied. The consensus is that it can affect all sub-systems of a language depending on the intensity of contact (see eg. Thomason & Kaufman 1988). The other type, less frequently noticed and only recently receiving attention (see eg. François 2011, Arnal 2011), is **contact-induced differentiation** (CID) where the change acts specifically to make the languages less similar. This type of contact-induced change predominantly affects the parts of a language which speakers are most conscious of being distinct: the phonological forms of morphemes and words.

It is hard to isolate contact-induced change in

related languages from the effects of common inheritance or normal independent drift. In languages in contact over a long period of time, it is impossible to tell whether the dropping of any single cognate is the result of chance variation or the action of a differentiation process. Likewise, if languages are compared using a single-valued measure of similarity (such as fraction of cognates in a Swadesh list), the effects of more or less contact-induced changes cannot be distinguished from a greater or lesser time-depth since the common ancestor. This is shown in figure 1.

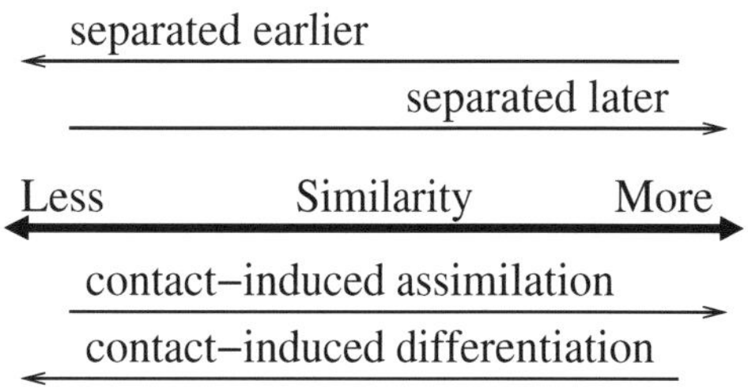

Figure 1: shows the problem of identifying contact-induced change between related languages. Contact-induced assimilation and having a more recent common ancestor can both account for language similarities. Contact-induced differentiation accounts for less similarity, but so does positing a remoter common ancestor that allows time for more independent drift resulting in greater differentiation without contact. A single similarity measure is insufficient to separate time-depth from contact-induced change.

Contact-induced change is, however, different from independent drift. If it is detectable at all, it will be because it creates different counts of synonyms and different proportions of cognates, than drift alone. Thus, with enough data, it should possible to distinguish the effects of time-depth and contact-induced change. This paper presents the results of a simulation to determine just how much data would be enough.

1.1 Overview

Section 2 discusses contact-induced change, and CID in particular. While it is easy to find instances of CIA, eg. borrowing a word from one language to another, it is harder to find unarguable cases of CID. They can be found, however, and some of these are discussed in section 2.2.

Section 3 describes language as a bundle of relations. Language changes can then be modelled as changes in these relations. A formal account of independent and contact-induced changes in relations is given, as the underpinnings for the next section.

This next section (section 4) investigates how much data is needed to develop 95% certainty that contact-induced change has occurred as opposed to independent change alone. As might be expected, the weaker the CIA or CID pressure, the more evidence needed to distinguish the types of change.

The final section considers the implications of the research, and situates it within a larger programme of investigation into contact-induced change.

1.2 Terminology

This paper uses terms from mathematics and linguistics. The term **relation** will only be used in its mathematical sense of a potentially many-to-many association from elements in one set, the **domain**, to elements in another, the **range**. An association between a domain element and a range element will be called a **link**. We introduce the term **doppels** to describe words from different languages which have had a common origin, or are so similar that they might be presumed to have a common origin. These differ from **cognates** in two ways. Although cognates must have had a common origin, doppels need not – they may just look like they do. Also, where there is a common origin, cognates must have evolved with the language as a whole, while doppels may be the result of borrowing. Etymologically, **doppel** is a doppel of the German **Doppel**, *duplicate, copy, double.*

2 Contact-Induced Change in Natural Languages

It is impossible to study language history without being aware of the impact of contact on languages all around the world, not least in the current age of globalisation. However, while the most transparent and best known process of contact-induced assimilation, word borrowing, has been a focus in historical linguistics, some other assimilatory phenomena and almost all differentiating processes are only recently receiving attention.

2.1 Contact-Induced Assimilation

Contact-induced assimilation (CIA) describes any process which causes two languages to become more similar. The increased similarity could be the result of: more doppels between the languages, due to one language borrowing from another; convergent phonology, as a large community of bilinguals use a single phonemic inventory for both languages; or convergent syntax and morphology. This last may occur as the speech of weak bilinguals, dropping rich morphology and using a lot of word-for-word translations in their non-native tongues, impacts the entire community.

English itself exemplifies the extent to which borrowing can make languages similar. Finkenstaedt and Wolff (1973) found that Latin and French (including Old Norman) have each contributed more words to Modern English than its Germanic parent language has. English speakers consequently often find it easier to learn a Romance language than a Germanic one.

Metatypy (Ross, 2006) is one type of contact-induced change at the grammatical level. Languages engaged in metatypy, such as Kannada and Marathi in the Indian village of Kupwar, can come to have (nearly) identical grammatical and morphological organisation; the languages only differ in their lexical forms. One result is that it is easy to translate from one language to the other, simply by replacing a morpheme in one language by its form in the other.

CIA seems to be much more common than CID. This may, however, be due to the fact that it is much easier to detect, because similarity is inherently less likely to occur by chance than dissimilarity.

2.2 Contact-Induced Differentiation

Because dissimilatory change is sometimes, but not always, hard to detect, many of the known cases of it arise because it is done deliberately and speakers report that they are doing it. Thomason (2007) gives two principal motivations for this kind of deliberate change: (a) a desire or need to increase the difference between one's own speech and someone else's, and (b) a desire or need to keep outsiders at a distance. However, the two recent studies already mentioned – François (2011) and Arnal (2011) – describe how this type of change may arise without "differentiation" per se being the primary motivation (see François 2011:229-30 in particular).

A situation that fits the first description is that found in one of the dialects of Lambayeque Quechua where speakers systematically distort their words in order to make their speech different from that of neighbouring dialects. One of the processes used involves the distortion of words by metathesis giving, for example: /yaw.ra/ from /yawar/, /-tqa/ from /taq/, /-psi/ from /pis/ and /kablata /from /kabalta/ (Thomason 2007:51). This kind of process clearly gives rise to a system with different phonotactics.

There is also anecdotal evidence that non-Castilian languages of the Iberian Peninsula have undergone deliberate differentiation. Wright (1998) reports that some late-medieval Portuguese avoided using words similar or identical to the corresponding Castilian words when a less similar synonym was available, while Vidal (1998) reports the same behaviour among the Catalan. More recently Arnal (2011) has described further differentiating change to Catalan lexical forms due to increased levels of Spanish/Catalan bilingualism among native Spanish speakers, following the establishment of Catalan as a co-official language in 1983. There have also been processes of differentiation at play in Galician, where purists have promoted alternatives to items shared with Castilian (Posner and Green, 1993; Beswick, 2007). These in turn are balanced by movements to assimilate Galician with Portuguese.

François (2011) describes the strong tendency for languages spoken in the Torres and Banks islands of northern Vanuatu to diverge in the forms of their words, resulting in a pattern where closely related languages that would be expected to have high levels of cognacy, instead exhibit highly distinctive vocabularies.

Perhaps the most extreme example of change aimed at increasing the difference in one's own speech is that of the Uisai dialect of Buin, a language spoken in Papua New Guinea on Bougainville island. Laycock (1982:34) reports that Uisai shows diametrically opposed noun categories to other dialects. The markers for category 1 in Uisai occur only with category 2 elsewhere, and vice-versa. In this particular parameter these dialects are significantly more different than would be expected by chance.

The desire to differentiate languages in this way doesn't necessarily imply hostility or antagonism. Laycock also reports an opinion from the Sepik region of Papua New Guinea: *it wouldn't be any good if we all talked the same, we like to know where people come from.*

One of the reasons for the current work is to create the tools which might let us see whether these efforts to change languages, for social or political reasons, actually have a lasting effect on the vocabulary, or whether they are at best ephemeral (see eg. Thomason & Kaufman 1988, Ross 2007, Aikhenvald 2002; and François 2011, Arnal 2011 on differentiation).

3 Evolutionary Change in Relations

In this section, we explore the formal model that we will use to distinguish normal, independent change from contact-induced change. The first step is to model languages as a bundle of relations. Modelling language in this way is not new, but is rarely made explicit.

3.1 Language as a Bundle of Relations

Much language structure can be expressed as relations between different spaces. For example, the lexicon can be regarded as a relation between the space of meanings available in a language and the phonological forms of morphemes expressing that meaning. There can be meanings represented by multiple forms, such as **ready** and **prepared**, or forms with multiple meanings such as **fire** in the sense of **burning** or **terminating employment**.

Another language relation maps phonemes-in-contexts to phones that can realise them. Phonemic distinctions may collapse in some contexts, such as with the final devoicing of obstruents in Polish, so that distinct phonemes are realised with the same phone. Likewise, the same phoneme, even in the one context, may be realised by multiple phones; the Portuguese phoneme /ʁ/ is realised as [ʁ], [ʀ], [ɣ] or even [r], with multiple possible realisations even for the one speaker.

So both the lexicon and phonetic realisation can be modelled with relations.

3.2 Primitive Changes on Relations

If some important language structures are relational, an interesting question is what sort of evolutionary changes can effect these relations. This subsection explores a number of minimal changes which can effect relations. To the best of our knowledge, this is the first time that language changes have been characterised this way. The starting point is a simple relation between a domain and a range, as shown in figure 2.

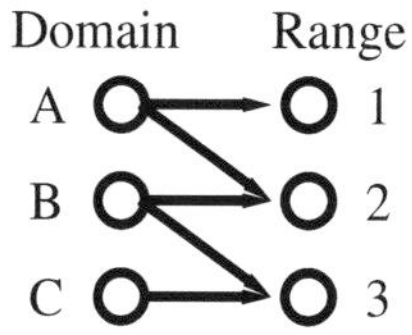

Figure 2: shows a relation from a small domain to a similarly-sized range.

The first kind of change is a global substitution, see figure 3. This is where a change of permutation or merger applies to elements of either the domain or the range. All of the pairs which contain the affected elements are modified, hence the name.

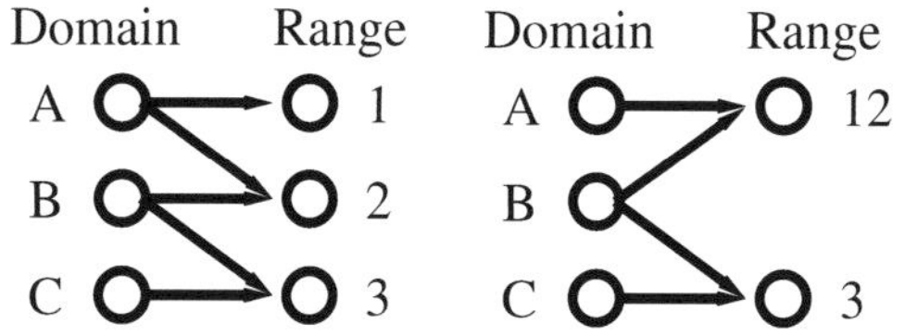

Figure 3: shows a global substitution: range elements 1 and 2 are merged, preserving all links. It is called a **global substitution** as every link with 1 or 2 in the range now has 12 as its range element.

Modifications of the phonetic relation can be of this kind. For example, when Gaelic – both Irish and Scottish – merged [ð] into [ɣ], the change affected both lexical /ð/ in closed class words, such as the preposition <dha>, /ða/, *to*, as well as lexical /ð/ in open class words such as <duine>, /duɲə/, *person*. This was a global substitution.

More frequently met are small changes, we will call **local mutations**. These involve either the insertion of a single link, or the deletion of a single link.

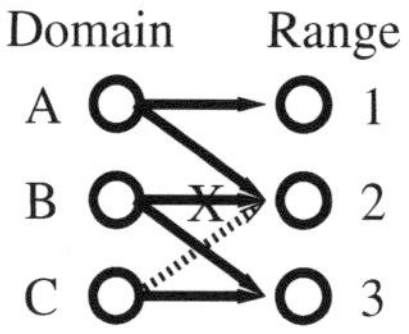

Figure 4: shows two separate local mutations in a relation: a deletion marked by an X on the link, and an insertion shown as a dotted arrow.

Gloabl changes can be expressed as local changes combined with relation composition.

The lexical relation associates meanings with the phonological forms, which may take the form phonemes in contexts. The phonemic map then projects these onto their phonetic realisations.

If a single link in the phoneme realisation map is dropped, then all lexical meanings expressed using that phoneme-in-context can no longer realise it with that phone. If a single link is added to the phonetic relation, then all lexical meanings expressed using that phoneme-in-context can now realise it with the new phone. This multiplier effect on changes means single sound changes can have a disproportionate effect on the similarity of cognate forms in two languages. Ellison and Kirby (2006) presented a similarity measure which bypasses this superficial difference: pairs of domain elements are compared for the similarity of the corresponding sets of range elements, and these similarity values are then compared cross-linguistically. This measure mitigates the effect of global substitutions.

The iterated application of local mutational changes to language structures is called **drift**. In traditional models of language history, it is the primary mechanism for explaining difference, while the shared parent language is the primary explanation of similarity.

3.3 Contact-induced change

So far, we have only looked at change arising in independent relations. Change, in language at least, is often the result of contact with the corresponding relational structure in another language. Figure 5 shows two relations between the same domain and range, superimposed. Later diagrams will use this same superimposed representation in describing contact-induced changes.

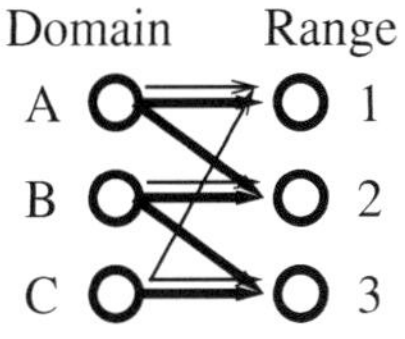

Figure 5: shows two relations simultaneously: the links from one are shown with thick arrows, those from the other with thin. Links common to both relations are doppels.

In considering contact-induced change, it is worth noting that the change need not be symmetrical between the languages involved. If one language is spoken by a dominant, larger population, it may see no reason to differentiate itself from the language of a smaller community. The smaller community may feel that language differentiation is a way to protect its identity. Whatever the reason, we shall call the relation undergoing differentiation the **assimilating** or **differentiating relation**, and the relation it is pushing away from, or pull towards, the **reference relation**.

Contact-induced assimilation or CIA can consist of the insertion of a new link into the relation, or the deletion of a link in the relation. As assimilation is about making the relations more similar, so insertion applies to create doppels where the reference relation has a link and the assimilating relation does not. Likewise assimilation applies to delete links where the reference relation does not have a link but the assimilating relation does. Examples of this kind of assimilation are shown in figure 6.

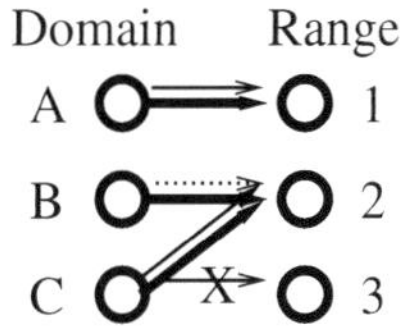

Figure 6: shows contact-induced assimilation (CIA) as an insertion shown as a dotted line and a deletion marked with an X. Existing links of the assimilating relation are shown thin, while those of the reference relation are shown thick. In CIA, links are more likely to be inserted to make a doppel, and deleted where no doppel exists.

The reverse is true in cases of contact-induced differentiation – see figure 7. The differentiating

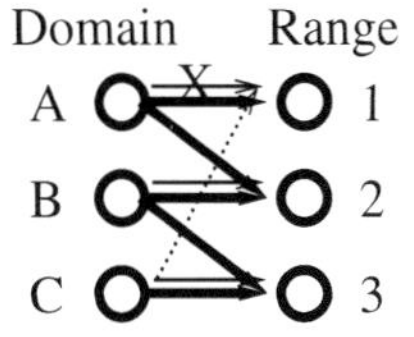

Figure 7: shows contact-induced differentiation (CID) in the form of an insertion shown as a dotted line and a deletion marked with an X. Existing links of the differentiating relation are shown thin, while those of the reference relation are shown thick. In CID, links are more likely to be deleted if they have a doppel, and inserted where they do not.

relation is more likely to delete a link which is half of a doppel than delete other links. Likewise, it is more likely to create a link where there is none in the reference relation, rather than borrow a link from it.

4 When can CIA/CID be Inferred?

This paper addresses the question: how much data is required to distinguish cases of contact-induced change from similarity due to a common ancestor and differences due to drift? The question will be addressed in terms of relations and the types of changes covered in section 3.2 and section 3.3. To render the problem tractable, we need an additional assumption about the lexical relations: they have the form described in section 4.1.

4.1 RPOFs

We restrict lexical relations to RPOFs. An **RPOF** is a **reverse of a partial onto function**, in other words, a relation such that each element of the domain participates in at least one link, while each element in the range participates in at most one link. An example of such a relation appears in figure 8. If the lexical relation in a language is

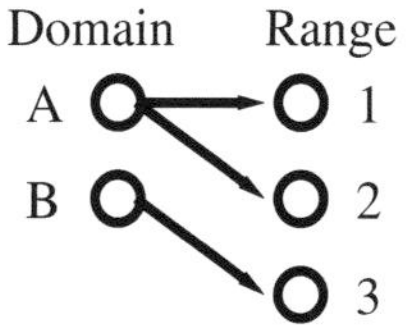

Figure 8: shows an RPOF relation. In RPOFs, each element of the domain has at least one link, while each element of the range has at most one link.

an RPOF, then each meaning is expressible with at least one morphemic form, and each potential form expresses exactly one meaning, or else is not used in the language. In other words, the language has no homophones.

This assumption is usually only mildly inaccurate. For some languages, however, such as Chinese, mono-syllabic morphemes are frequently homophonous. The analysis presented here may fail for languages of this kind.

The advantage of using RPOFs is that their structure can be summarised by a cardinality function – a partial function from natural numbers to natural numbers. This function associates with any cardinality of range subset the number of elements of the domain which associate with a range set of exactly that size. For example, the relation shown in figure 8 maps one input onto two outputs, while it maps the second input to a single output. Thus its cardinality function is $\{2 : 1, 1 : 1\}$. Such specifications completely characterise an RPOF relation upto permutation of either the domain or range.

One of the effects of assuming RPOF structure for the lexical relation is that we do not allow the sole link from any domain element to undergo deletion. This is because all domain elements must retain at least a single link. For the lexical relation, this has the fairly likely consequence that the sole morpheme representing a meaning is unlikely to be lost, while if there are multiple synonyms, one might fall out of use.

4.2 Pairs of RPOFs

When we are comparing RPOFs evolved from a common parent, we can characterise their relationship, upto permutation of the domain and range, by frequency counts over triples. The triples are numbers describing how many elements of the range a domain element links to: solely in relation 1, in both relations (ie, the number of doppels), and solely in relation 2. For each triple, we count the number of domain elements which have the correspondingly sized projections on the range. This kind of summarisation allows us to describe the similarity of two lexical relations with a few hundred numbers if we limit ourselves to, say, domain elements linking to at most 10 range elements in either relation.

4.3 Significance Testing

It easy to evaluate the posterior likelihood of a set of data associating a counting number with each triple, $D \in \mathbb{N}^{Triples}$, given a model $M \in Dist(Triples)$ in the form of a distribution over triples. The triple associated with each domain element is assumed to be the result of independent processes – in other words, we assume that the number of doppel and non-doppel forms associated with a meaning is independent of the numbers associated with other meanings.

$$P(D|M) = \prod_{t \in Triples} M(t)^{D(t)}$$

We can evaluate the likelihood of one model M_1 generating data at the frequencies produced by a second model M_2. The posterior probability of the data relative to the second model is shown in equation (1), while the probability of generating that data from the model which did indeed generate it is shown in equation (2).

$$P(M_2|M_1) = \prod_{t \in Triples} M_1(t)^{M_2(t)} \quad (1)$$

$$P(M_2|M_2) = \prod_{t \in Triples} M_2(t)^{M_2(t)} \quad (2)$$

The likelihood ratio, i.e. the ratio of posterior likelihoods of M_2 and M_1, is shown in equation (3).

$$\frac{P(M_2|M_1)}{P(M_2|M_2)} = \prod_{t \in Triples} \frac{M_1(t)}{M_2(t)}^{M_2(t)} \quad (3)$$

This ratio expresses the amount of information we are likely to gain about which distribution is correct as a result of looking at a single data item. In terms of RPOF relations, this single data item is the triple of counts for relation-1-only, doppels, and relation-2-only associated with a meaning. If, as assumed above, the counts associated with each domain element are independent, then the likelihood ratio is raised to the power of the number N of items seen.

$$\frac{P(M_2|M_1)}{P(M_2|M_2)}^N = [\prod_{t \in Triples} \frac{M_1(t)}{M_2(t)}^{M_2(t)}]^N \quad (4)$$

To establish a chance prediction at $p < 0.05$, we merely need to know that $P(M_2|M_1) < P(M_2|M_2)$, and then determine the minimum level of N for which the ratio in equation (4) is less than $1/19$. This number of items generated from the target distribution would allow it to be distinguished from chance at a ratio of 19 : 1.

Determining the correct value for N here is a general problem known as **power analysis**. For standard experimental designs and corresponding statistics, the power analysis can be found in many texts, such as that by (Bausell and Li, 2006), and many computing libraries such as the **pwr** library for power analysis in R (see `http://cran.r-project.org/web/packages/pwr/`). Where the model design is as complex as that described here, the power analysis must be constructed from first principles.

It is often easier to work with this quantity in informational rather than probabilistic form, where it takes the form shown in equation (5).

$$-\log \frac{P(M_2|M_1)}{P(M_2|M_2)} = -\sum_{t \in Triples} M_2(t) \log \frac{M_1(t)}{M_2(t)} \quad (5)$$

The quantity in equation (5) is the well-known **Kullback-Liebler divergence** $D_{KL}(M_2||M_1)$ of the two distributions, also known as the **discrimination information**. Significance is achieved when this value multiplied by the number of data items is greater than $log_2(19) = 4.2479$.

4.4 Models with and without Context-Induced Change

The construction of the no-CIA/CID and the with-CIA/CID distributions makes use of four parameters.

In the non-context model:

> **insertion** of a link combines the probability α of making a change at all for any given domain element, with the probability $\beta/(1+\beta)$ that the change will be the addition rather than deletion of a link, into a likelihood of adding a link per domain element of $\alpha\beta/(1+\beta)$.

> **deletion** of a link combines the probability α of making a change at all for any given domain element, with the probability $1.0/(1+\beta)$ that the change will be to a deletion, with the number m of links to select from for that domain element, so the probability of deleting any of those links is $\alpha/(m + m\beta)$.

In the case of CIA/CID, we only consider the impact of contact on deletion. The per-link probability of deletion $\alpha/(m + m\beta)$ is modified by a parameter γ indicating how strong the effects of contact are. Positive γ brings about CIA – with shared links less likely to be dropped than others, while negative γ develops CID – shared links are more likely to be dropped than others. The probability of dropping any given doppel link from a given range node is $(1-\gamma)z$, and of any unshared link is z where n_d is the number of doppel links from the domain element, and n_u the number of unshared links in the differentiating relation, and z is given in equation (6).

$$z = \frac{\alpha}{((1-\gamma)n_d + n_u)(1+\beta)} \quad (6)$$

4.5 Simulation Results

The above model was used to generate distributions over triples for non-CIA/CID relation pairs, and relation pairs with additional CIA/CID processes. The number of iterations of the mutation process with or without CIA/CID was fixed at 100 in creating the generating distribution M_2. The parameter α was fixed at 0.1 and β at 0.5. The value for β was chosen to approximately reproduce the single-language distribution of range-set sizes for Castillian as computed from the Spanish wordnet. The bias parameter γ was varied from -0.5 to 0.5 in steps of 0.1. For each level of bias, a search was made over non-CIA/CID distributions at different depths from the common ancestor – this is the parameter N – until the distribution with the least K-L divergence from the generated distribution was found. This found distribution M_1 represents the null hypothesis, that the data arose without CIA/CID bias.

The number of data items needed to achieve significant recognition of the presence of CIA/CID bias is $4.2479/D_{KL}(M_1||M_2)$. The results for various levels of γ are shown in figure 9.

γ	N	S	D
-0.5	118	3128	0.091
-0.4	115	4364	0.096
-0.3	111	6839	0.101
-0.2	108	13800	0.107
-0.1	104	47378	0.114
0.1	95	30913	0.133
0.2	90	7331	0.145
0.3	85	2793	0.160
0.4	79	1278	0.178
0.5	72	654	0.203

Figure 9: Tabulation of number S of data items needed to achieve significance and the number of iterations N of the best non-CIA/CID model, and fraction of doppels remaining D, against CIA/CID bias parameter γ. Note that fewer data items are needed to recognise significant assimilatory bias (positive values for γ) than differentiating bias (negative values of γ) at the same strength.

5 Conclusion

This paper has looked at different ways that relations may evolve from a common parent structure. They may undergo local mutational changes, global substitutions, independent changes, or those triggered by contact with other relations. In one class of relations, with reasonable assumptions, it is clear that a large, but possible, amount of data needs to be adduced to ascertain that CIA and/or CID have occured, rather than just shared origin and independent drift.

In historical linguistics, this opens the door, for testing whether the impressionistic accounts of CID are reflected in the distributional properties of the languages concerned. It may also be possible to circumvent the onerous data requirements, by bringing in data from multiple independent relations within the language, such as those defining morphological structure and phonology, as well as the lexicon.

As mentioned in the introduction, this work is part of a larger programme by the authors to develop statistical tools able to show that CID has taken place, if it has. This work is partly driven by the need to account historically for the low cognacy but high structural similarity between nearby Australian languages. In the Daly River area, adjacent languages with very similar phonology, syntax and morphology show remarkably low cognacy counts, often around 8% (Harvey, 2008). One possible explanation for this is a powerful CID imperative acting over a short time depth to differentiate the vocabularies of the languages. The result presented in this paper suggests that with sufficient lexical data, direct statistical evidence could be found if this is indeed the correct explanation.

There are potential uses for this work beyond historical linguistics as well. The model might assist in some cases of plagiarism detection, for example, where two students worked together on an assignment, and then set out to deliberately differentiate them by altering vocabulary. Similar analysis of documents might reflect other reasons for reworking a text, such as to give it a new identity for a new setting.

References

A. Aikhenvald. 2002. *Language contact in Amazonia*. Oxford University Press, Oxford.

Antoni Arnal. 2011. Linguistic changes in the catalan spoken in catalonia under new contact conditions. *Journal of Language Contact*, 4:5–25.

R. Barker Bausell and Yu-Fang Li. 2006. *Power Analysis for Experimental Research: A Practical Guide for the Biological, Medical and Social Sciences*. Cambridge University Press, March.

Jaine E. Beswick. 2007. *Regional nationalism in Spain: language use and ethnic identity in Galicia*. Multilingual Matters.

Karl Brugmann. 1884. Zur frage nach den verwandtschaftverhltnissen der indogermanischen sprachen. *Internationale Zeitschrift fr allgemeine Sprachwissenschaft*, 1:226–56.

T. Mark Ellison and Simon Kirby. 2006. Measuring language divergence by intra-lexical comparison. In *ACL*, pages 273–80, Sydney.

Thomas Finkenstaedt and Dieter Wolff. 1973. *Ordered profusion: studies in dictionaries and the English lexicon*. C Winter.

Alexandre François. 2011. Social ecology and language history in the northern vanuatu linkage: a tale of divergence and convergence. *Journal of Historical Linguistics*, 1:175–246.

Mark Harvey. 2008. *Proto-Mirndi: a discontinuous language family in northern Australia*. Pacific Linguistics, Canberra.

Sir William Jones. 1786. The third anniversary discourse, delivered 2nd february, 1786: on the hindus. *Asiatick Researches*, 1:415–31.

Donald C. Laycock. 1982. Melanesian linguistic diversity: a melanesian choice? In R.J. May and H. Nelson, editors, *Melanesia: beyond diversity*, pages 33–38. Australian National University Press, Canberra.

Rebecca Posner and John N. Green. 1993. *Bilingualism and Linguistic Conflict in Romance*. Walter de Gruyter.

Malcolm D. Ross. 2006. Metatypy. In K. Brown, editor, *Encylcopedia of language and linguistics*. Elsevier, Oxford, 2nd ed edition.

Malcolm Ross. 2007. Calquing and metatypy. *Journal of Language Contact, Thema*, 1:116–43.

August Schleicher. 1861. *Compendium der vergleichenden Grammatik der indogermanischen Sprachen*. Hermann Bhlau, Weimar.

Sarah Grey Thomason and Terrence Kaufman. 1988. *Language contact, creolization, and genetic linguistics*. University of California Press, Berkeley & Los Angeles.

Sarah Grey Thomason. 2007. Language contact and deliberate change. *Journal of Language Contact, Thema*, 1:41–62.

Carrasquer Vidal. 1998. Untitled post in 'Cladistic language concepts' thread, HISTLING mailing list, Oct.

Roger Wright. 1998. Untitled post in 'Cladistic language concepts' thread, HISTLING mailing list, Oct.

Empiricist Solutions to Nativist Puzzles by means of Unsupervised TSG

Rens Bod
Institute for Logic, Language & Computation
University of Amsterdam
Science Park 904, 1098XH Amsterdam, NL
rens.bod@uva.nl

Margaux Smets
Institute for Logic, Language & Computation
University of Amsterdam
Science Park 904, 1098XH Amsterdam, NL
margauxsmets@gmail.com

Abstract

While the debate between nativism and empiricism exists since several decades, surprisingly few common learning problems have been proposed for assessing the two opposing views. Most empiricist researchers have focused on a relatively small number of linguistic problems, such as *Auxiliary Fronting* or *Anaphoric One*. In the current paper we extend the number of common test cases to a much larger series of problems related to *wh-questions, relative clause formation, topicalization, extraposition from NP* and *left dislocation*. We show that these hard cases can be empirically solved by an unsupervised tree-substitution grammar inferred from child-directed input in the Adam corpus (Childes database).

1 Nativism versus Empiricism

How much knowledge of language is innate and how much is learned through experience? The *nativist* view endorses that there is an innate language-specific component and that human language acquisition is guided by innate rules and constraints ("Universal Grammar"). The *empiricist* view assumes that there is no language-specific component and that language acquisition is the product of abstractions from empirical input by means of general cognitive capabilities. Despite the apparent opposition between these two views, the essence of the debate lies often in the relative contribution of prior knowledge and linguistic experience (cf. Lidz et al. 2003; Clark and Lappin 2011; Ambridge & Lieven 2011). Following the nativist view, the linguistic evidence is so hopelessly underdetermined that innate components are necessary. This Argument from the Poverty of the Stimulus can be phrased as follows (see Pullum & Scholz 2002 for a detailed discussion):

(i) Children acquire a certain linguistic phenomenon
(ii) The linguistic input does not give enough evidence for acquiring the phenomenon
(iii) There has to be an innate component for the phenomenon

In this paper we will falsify step (ii) for a large number of linguistic phenomena that have been considered "parade cases" of innate constraints (Crain 1991; Adger 2003; Crain and Thornton 2006). We will show that even if a linguistic phenomenon is *not* in a child's input, it can be learned by an 'ideal' learner from a tiny fraction of child-directed utterances, namely by combining fragments from these utterances using the Adam corpus in the Childes database (MacWhinney 2000).

Previous work on empirically solving nativist puzzles, focused on a relatively small set of phenomena such as *auxiliary fronting* (Reali & Christiansen 2005; Clark and Eyraud 2006) and *Anaphoric One* (Foraker et al. 2009). Some of the proposed solutions were based on linear models, such as trigram models (Reali & Christiansen 2005), though Kam et al. (2008) showed that the success of these models depend on accidental English facts. Other empiricist approaches have taken the notion of structural dependency together with a combination operation as minimal requirements (e.g. Bod 2009), which overcomes the problems raised by Kam et al. (2008). Yet, it remains an open question which of the many other syntactic phenomena in the nativist literature can be acquired by such a general learning method on the basis of child-directed speech.

In this paper we will deal with a much larger set of problems than used before in empiricist computational models. These problems are well-known in the generativist literature (e.g. Ross 1967; Adger 2003; Borsley 2004) and are related to *wh-questions, relative clause formation, topicalization, extraposition* and *left dislocation*. It turns out that these hard cases can be learned by a simple unsupervised grammar induction algorithm that returns the sentence with the best-ranked derivation for a particular phenomenon, using only a very small fraction of the input a child receives.

2 Methodology

Our methodology is very simple: by means of an induced Tree-Substitution Grammar or TSG (see Bod 2009 for an in-depth study), we compute from the alternative sentences of a syntactic phenomenon reported in the generativist literature -- see below -- the sentence with the *best-ranked shortest derivation* (see Section 3) according to the unsupervised TSG. Next, we check whether this sentence corresponds with the grammatical sentence.

For example, given a typical nativist problem like auxiliary fronting, the question is: how do we choose the correct sentence from among the alternatives (0) to (2):

(0) Is the boy who is eating hungry?
(1) *Is the boy who eating is hungry?
(2) *Is the boy who is eating is hungry?

According to Adger (2003), Crain (1991) and others, this phenomenon is regulated by an innate principle. In our empiricist approach, instead, we parse all three sentences by our TSG. Next, the sentence with the best-ranked shortest derivation is compared with the grammatical expression.

Ideally, rather than selecting from given sentences, we would like to have a model that starts with a certain meaning representation for which next the best sentence is generated. In the absence of such a semantic component, we let our model select directly from the set of possible sentences as they are provided in the literature as alternatives, where we will mostly focus on the classical work by Ross (1967) supplemented by the more recent work of Adger (2003) and Borsley (2004). In section 9 we will discuss the shortcomings of our approach and suggest some improvements for future research.

3 Grammar induction with TSG: the best-ranked k-shortest derivation

For our induced grammar, we use the formalism of Tree-Substitution Grammar. This formalism has recently generated considerable interest in the field of grammar induction (e.g. Bod 2006; O'Donnell et al. 2009; Post and Gildea 2009; Cohn et al. 2010). As noted by Cohn et al. (2010) and others, this formalism has a number of advantages. For example, *its productive units (elementary trees of arbitrary size) allow for both structural and lexical sensitivity* (see Bod et al. 2003), while grammars in this formalism are still efficiently learnable from a corpus of sentences in cubic time and space.

As an example, figure 1 gives two TSG derivations and parse trees for the sentence *She saw the dress with the telescope*. Note that the first derivation corresponds to the shortest derivation, as it consists of only two elementary trees.

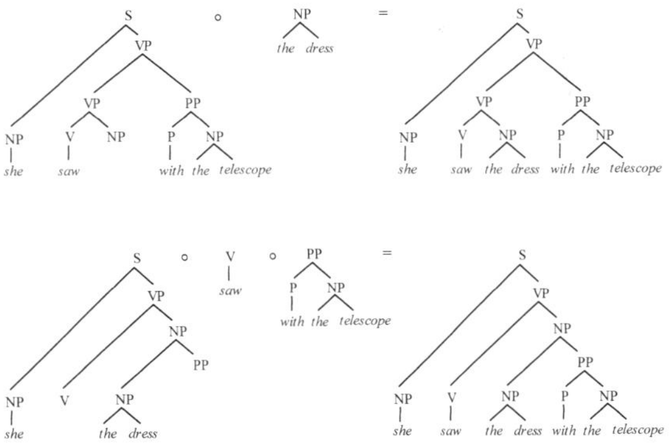

Figure 1. Two TSG derivations, resulting in different parse trees, for the sentence *She saw the dress with the telescope*

Our induction algorithm is similar to Bod (2006) where first, all binary trees are assigned to a set of sentences, and next, the relative frequencies of the subtrees in the binary trees (using a PCFG reduction, see below) are used to compute the most probable trees. While we will use Bod's method of assigning all binary trees to a set of sentences, we will not compute the most probable tree or sentence. Instead we compute the k-shortest derivations for each sentence after which the sum of ranks of the subtrees in the k derivations determines the *best-ranked shortest derivation* (Bod 2000). This last step is important, since the shortest derivation alone is known to perform poorly (Bansal and Klein 2011). In Zollmann and Sima'an (2005) it is shown that training by means of shortest derivations corresponds to maximum likelihood training in the limit if the corpus grows to infinity.

Our approach to focus on the k shortest derivation rather than the most probable tree or most probable sentence is partly motivated by our different task: it is well-known that the probability of a sentence decreases exponentially with sentence length. This is problematic since, when choosing among alternative sentences, the longest sentence may be (the most) grammatical. Instead, by focusing on the (k-) *shortest derivations* this problem can – at least partly – be overcome.

From an abstract level, our grammar induction algorithm works as follows (see also Zollmann and Sima'an 2005). Given a corpus of sentences:

1. Divide the corpus into a 50% Extraction Corpus (EC) and a 50% Held out Corpus (HC).
2. Assign all unlabeled binary trees to the sentences in EC and store them in a parse forest.
3. Convert the subtrees from the parse forests into a compact PCFG reduction (Goodman 2003).
4. Compute the k-shortest derivations for the sentences in HC using the PCFG reduction.
5. Compute the *best-ranked derivation* for each sentence by the sum of the ranks of the subtrees (where the most frequent subtrees get rank 1, next most frequent subtrees get rank 2, etc., thus the best-ranked derivation is the one with the lowest total score).
6. Use the subtrees in the trees generated by the best-ranked derivations to form the TSG (following Zollmann & Sima'an 2005).

The learning algorithm above does not induce POS-tags. In fact, in our experiments below we test directly on POS-strings. This makes sense because the nativist constraints are also defined on categories of words, and not on specific sentences. Of course, future work should also parse directly with word strings instead of with POS strings (for which unsupervised POS-taggers may be used).

Rather than using the (exponentially many) subtrees from the binary trees to construct our TSG, we convert them into a more compact homomorphic PCFG. We employ Goodman's reduction method where each node in a tree is converted into exactly 8 PCFG rules (Goodman 2003). This PCFG reduction is linear in the number of nodes in the corpus (Goodman 2003, pp. 130-133).

The k-shortest derivations can be computed by Viterbi by assigning each elementary tree equal probability (Bod 2000). We follow the third algorithm in Huang and Chiang (2005), where first a traditional Viterbi-chart is created, which enumerates in an efficient way all possible subderivations. Next, the algorithm starts at the root node and recursively looks for the k-best derivations, where we used k = 100. In addition, we employed the size reduction technique developed in Teichmann (2011) for U-DOP/TSG.

We used all 12K child-*directed* utterances in the Adam corpus from the Childes database (MacWhinney 2000). These utterances come with POS-tags, which were stripped off the sentences and fed to our TSG induction algorithm. The child-directed sentences were randomly split into 50% EC and 50% HC. The subtrees from EC were used to derive a TSG for the POS-strings from HC. The resulting TSG consisted of 914,744 different subtrees. No smoothing was used. With the methodology explained in Section 2, we used this TSG to test against a number of well-known nativist problems from the literature (Ross 1967; Adger 2003).

It may be important to stress that the Adam corpus is based on only 2 hours of recordings per fortnight. This corresponds to just a tiny fraction of the total number of utterances heard by Adam. Thus our TSG has access only to this very small fraction of Adam's linguistic input, and we do not assume that our model (let alone a child) literally stores all previously heard utterances.

4 The problem of wh-questions

The study of wh-questions or wh-movement is one of oldest in syntactic theory (Ross 1967) and is usually dealt with by a specific set of "island constraints", where islands are constituents out of which wh-elements cannot move. These constraints are incorporated in the more recent Minimalist framework (Adger 2003, pp. 389ff). Of course, our goal is different from Minimalism (or generative grammar in general). Rather than trying to explain the phenomenon by separate constraints, we try to model them by just one, more general constraint: the best-ranked (k-shortest) derivation. We do not intend to show that the constraints proposed by Ross, Adger and others are incorrect. We want to demonstrate that these constraints can also be modeled by a more *general* principle. Additionally, we intend to show that the phenomena related to wh-questions can be modeled by using only a tiny fraction of child-directed speech.

4.1 Unbounded scope of wh-questions

First of all we must account for the seemingly unbounded scope of wh-movement: wh-questions can have infinitely deep levels of embedding. The puzzle lies in the fact that children only hear constructions of level 1, e.g. (3), but how then is it possible that they can generalize (certainly as adults) this simple construction to more complex ones of levels 2 and 3 (e.g. (4) and (5))?

(3) who did you steal from?
(4) who did he say you stole from?
(5) who did he want her to say you stole from?

The initial nativist answer developed by Ross (1967) was to introduce a transformational rule with variables, and in the more recent Minimalist framework it is explained by a complex interplay between the so-called Phase Impenetrability Constraint and the Feature Checking Requirement (Adger 2003).

Our model proposes instead to build constructions like (4) and (5) by simply using fragments children heard before. When we let our induced TSG parse sentence (3), we obtain the following derivation consisting of 3 subtrees (where the operation 'o' stands for leftmost node substitution of TSG-subtrees). For reasons of space, we represent the unlabeled subtrees by squared brackets, and for reasons of readability we substitute the POS-tags with the words. (As mentioned above we trained and tested only with POS-strings.)

[X [who [X [did X]]] o [X [X from]] o [X [you steal]] =

[X [who [X [did [X [[X [you steal]] from]]]]]

Although this derivation is *not* the shortest one in terms of number of subtrees, it obtained the best ranking (sum of subtree ranks) among the 100-shortest derivations. In fact, the derivation above consists of three highly frequent subtrees with (respective) ranking of 1,153 + 7 + 488 = 1,648. The absolute shortest derivation (k=1) consisted of only one subtree (i.e. the entire tree) but had a ranking of 26,223.

Sentences (4) and (5) could also be parsed by combinations of three subtrees, which in this case were also the shortest derivations. The following is the shortest derivation for (4):

[X [who [X [did he say X]]] o [X [X from]] o [X [you stole]] =

[X [who [X [did he say [X [[X [you stole]] from]]]]]

It is important to note that when looking at the speech produced by Adam himself, he only produced (3) but not (4) and (5) – and neither had he heard these sentences as a whole. It thus turns out that our induced TSG can deal with the presumed unbounded scope of wh-questions on the basis of simple combination of fragments heard before.

4.2 Complex NP constraint

The first constraint-related problem we deal with is the difference in grammaticality between sentences (4), (5) and (6), (7):

(6) *who did you he say stole from?
(7) * who did you he want her to say stole from?

The question usually posed is: how do children know that they can generalize from what they hear in sentence (3) to sentences (4) and (5) but not to (6) and (7). This phenomenon is dealt with in generative grammar by introducing a specific restriction: the complex NP constraint (see Adger 2003). But we can also solve it by the best-ranked derivation. To do so, we compare sentences with the same level of embedding, i.e. (4) and (6), both of level 2, and (5) and (7), of level 3. We thus view respectively (4), (6) and (5), (7) as competing expressions.

It turns out that (6) like (4) can be derived by minimally 3 subtrees, but with a worse ranking score. Similarly, (7) can also be derived by minimally 3 subtrees with a worse ranking score than (5). Since we tested on POS-strings, the result holds not only for these sentences of respective levels 2 and 3, but for all sentences of this type. Thus rather than assuming that the complex NP constraint must be innate, it can be modelled by recombining fragments from a fraction of previous utterances on the basis of the best-ranked derivation.

4.3 Left branch condition

The second wh-phenomenon we will look into is known as the Left Branch Condition (Ross 1967; Adger 2003). This condition has to do with the difference in grammaticality between (8) and (9):

(8) which book did you read?
(9) *which did you read book?

When we let our TSG parse these two sentences, we get the respective derivations (8') and (9'), where for reasons of readability we now give the substree-yields only:

(8') [X you read] o [which X] o [book did]

ranking: 608 + 743 + 8,708 = 10,059

(9') [which did X] o [you read book]

ranking: 12,809 + 1 = 12,810

Here we thus have a situation that, when looking at the 100-best derivations, the subtree ranking overrules the shortest derivation: although (9') is shorter than (8'), the rank of (8') nevertheless overrules (9'), leading to the correct alternative. Of course, it has to be seen whether this perhaps coincidentally positive result can be confirmed on other child-directed corpora.

4.4 Subject wh-questions

An issue that is not considered in early work on wh-questions (such as Ross 1967), but covered in the minimalist framework is the phenomenon that arises with subject wh-questions. We have to explain how children know that (10) is the grammatical way of asking the particular question, and (11), (12) and (13) are not.

(10) who kissed Bella
(11) *kissed who Bella
(12) *did who kiss Bella
(13) *who did kiss Bella

When we let our model parse these sentences, we obtain the following four derivations (where we give again only the subtree-yields):

(10') [who X] o [kissed Bella]

ranking: 22 + 6,694 = 6,716

(11') [X Bella] o [kissed who]

ranking: 24 + 6,978 = 7,002

(12') [did X Bella] o [who kiss]

ranking: 4,230 + 8,527 = 12,757

(13') [X kiss Bella] o [who did]

ranking: 4,636 + 2,563 = 7,199

Although all derivations are equally short, the best (= lowest) ranking score prefers the correct alternative.

4.5 Other wh-constraints modelled empirically

Besides the constraints given above, there are various other constraints related to wh-questions. These include:

- Sentential Subject Constraint
- WH-questions in situ
- Embedded WH-questions
- WH-islands
- Superiority
- Coordinate Structure Constraint

All but one of these constraints could be correctly modelled by our TSG, preferring the correct alternative on the basis of the best-ranked derivation and a fraction of a child's input. The only exception is the Coordinate Structure Constraint, as in (14) and (15):

(14) you love chicken and what?
(15) *what do you love chicken and?

Contrary to the ungrammaticality of (15), our TSG parser assigned the best rank to the derivation of (15). Of course it has to be seen how our TSG would perform on a corpus that is larger than Adam. Moreover, we will see that our TSG can correctly model the Coordinate Structure Constraint for other phenomena, even on the basis of the Adam corpus.

5 The problem of Relative clause formation

A phenomenon closely related to wh-questions is relative clause formation. As in 4.2, generativist/nativist approaches use the same complex NP constraint to distinguish between the grammatical sentence (16) and the ungrammatical sentence (17). The complex NP constraint is in fact believed to be universal.

(16) the vampire who I read a book about is dangerous
(17) *the vampire who I read a book which was about is dangerous

In (16), the ‘moved’ phrase `the vampire' is taken out of the non-complex NP `a book about <the vampire>; in (17), however, `the vampire' is ‘moved’ out of the complex NP `a book which was about <the vampire>’, which is not allowed.

Yet our TSG could also predict the correct alternative by means of the best ranked derivation alone, by respectively derivations (16’) and (17’):

(16’) [the vampire X is dangerous] o [who I read X] o [a book about]

ranking: 1,585,992 + 123,195 + 5,719 = 1,714,906

(17’) [the vampire X is dangerous] o [who I read X] o [a book which X] o [was about]

ranking: 1,585,992 + 123,195 + 184,665 + 12,745 = 1,906,597

Besides the complex NP constraint, the phenomenon of relative clause formation also uses most other constraints related to wh-questions: Left branch condition, Sentential Subject Constraint and Coordinate Structure Constraint. All these constraints could be modelled with the best-ranked derivation – this time including Coordinate structures (as e.g. (18) and (19)) that were unsuccessfully predicted by our TSG for wh-questions.

(18) Bella loves vampires and werewolves who are unstable
(19) *werewolves who Bella loves vampires and are unstable

6 The problem of Extraposition from NP

A problematic case for many nativist approaches is the so-called “Extraposition from NP” problem for which only ad hoc solutions exist. None of the constraints previously mentioned can explain (20) and (21):

(20) that Jacob picked Bella up who loves Edward is possible
(21) *that Jacob picked Bella up is possible who loves Edward

As Ross (1967), Borsley (2004) and others note, the Complex NP Constraint cannot explain (20) and (21), because it applies to elements of a sentence dominated by an NP, and here the moved constituent `who loves Edward' is a sentence dominated by an NP. Therefore, an additional concept needs to be introduced: `upward boundedness', where a rule is said to be upward bounded if elements moved by that rule cannot be moved over the boundaries of the first sentence above the elements being operated on (Ross 1967; Borsley 2004).

Thus additional machinery is needed to explain the phenomenon of Extraposition from NP. Instead, our notion of best ranked derivation needs no additional machinery and can do the job, as shown by derivations (20’) and (21’):

(20’) [X is possible] o [that Jacob picked X] o [Bella up X] o [who loves Edward]

ranking: 175 + 465,494 + 149,372 + 465,494 = 1,080,535

(21’) [X is possible X] o [that Jacob picked X] o [Bella up] o [who loves Edward] ranking: 3,257 + 465,494 + 176,910 + 465,494 = 1,111,155

7 The problem of Topicalization

Also the phenomenon of Topicalization is supposed to follow the Complex NP constraint, Left branch condition, Sentential Subject Constraint and Coordinate Structure Constraint, all of which can again be modelled by the best ranked derivation. For example, the topicalization in (22) is fine but in (23) it is not.

(22) Stephenie's book I read
(23) * Stephenie's I read book

Our TSG predicts the correct alternative by means of the best ranked derivation:

(22') [X I read] o [Stephenie's book]

ranking: 608 + 2,784 = 3,392

(23') [Stephenie's X book] o [I read]

ranking: 3,139 + 488 = 3,627

8 The problem of Left dislocation

The phenomenon of Left dislocation provides a particular challenge to nativist approaches since it shows that there are grammatical sentences that do not obey the Coordinate Structure Constraint (see Adger 2003; Borsley 2004). A restriction that is mentioned but not explained by Ross (1967), is the fact that in Left dislocation the moved constituent must be moved to the left of the main clause. Instead, movement merely to the left of a subordinate clause results in an ungrammatical sentence. For example, (24) is grammatical, because `Edward' is moved to the left of the main clause. Sentence (25), on the other hand, is ungrammatical, because `Edward' is only moved to the left of the subordinate clause `that you love <Edward>'.

(24) Edward, that you love him is obvious
(25) *that Edward, you love him is obvious

Our TSG has no problem in distinguishing between these two alternatives, as is shown below:

(24') [Edward X is obvious] o [that you love him]

ranking: 590,659 + 57,785 = 648,444

(25') [that X is obvious] o [Edward you love him]

ranking: 876,625 + 415,940 = 1,292,565

9 Discussion and conclusion

We have shown that an unsupervised TSG can capture virtually all phenomena related to wh-questions in a simple and uniform way. Furthermore, we have shown that our model can be extended to cover other phenomena, even phenomena that fall out of the scope of the traditional nativist account. Hence, for at least these phenomena, Arguments from Poverty of Stimulus can no longer be invoked. That is, step (ii) in Section 1 where it is claimed that children cannot learn the phenomenon on the basis of input alone, is refuted.

Phenomenon	**Succesful?**
Subject Auxiliary Fronting	yes
WH-Questions	
Unbounded Scope	yes
Complex NP Constraint	yes
Coordinate Structure Constraint	no
Left Branch Condition	yes
Subject WH-questions	yes
WH in situ	yes
Superiority	yes
Extended Superiority	yes
Embedded WH-questions	yes
WH-islands	yes
Relative Clause Formation	
Complex NP Constraint	yes
Coordinate Structure Constraint	yes
Sentential Subject Constraint	yes
Left Branch Condition	yes
Extraposition from NP	yes
Topicalization	
Complex NP Constraint	yes
Coordinate Structure Constraint	yes
Sentential Subject Constraint	yes
Left Branch Condition	yes
Left Dislocation	
Coordinate Structure Constraint	yes
Restriction	yes

Table 1. Overview of empiricist solutions to nativist problems tested so far (using as input the child-directed sentences in the Adam corpus of the Childes database), and whether they were successful.

Table 1 gives an overview of all phenomena we have tested so far with our model, and whether they can be successfully explained by the best-ranked k-shortest derivation (not all of these phenomena could be explicitly dealt with in the current paper).

Previous empiricist computational models that dealt with learning linguistic phenomena typically focused on auxiliary fronting (and sometimes on a couple of other problems – see Clark and Eyraud 2006). MacWhinney (2004) also describes ways to model some other language phenomena empirically, but this has not resulted into a computational framework. To the best of our knowledge, ours is the first empiricist computational model that also deals with the problems of wh-questions, relative clause formation, topicalization, extraposition from NP and left dislocation.

Many other computational models of language learning focus either on inducing syntactic structure (e.g. Klein and Manning 2005), or on evaluating which sentences can be generated by a model with which precision and recall (e.g. Bannard et al. 2009; Waterfall et al. 2010). Yet that work leaves the presumed 'hard cases' from the generativist literature untouched. This may be explained by the fact that most empiricist models do not deal with the concept of (absolute) grammaticality, which is a central concept in the generativist framework. It may therefore seem that the two opposing approaches are incommensurable. But this is only partly so: most empiricist models do have an implicit notion of relative grammaticality or some other ranking method for sentences and their structures. In some cases, like our model, the top-ranking can simply be equated with the notion of grammaticality. In this way empiricist and generativist models *can* be evaluated on the same problems.

There remains a question what our unsupervised TSG then exactly explains. It may be quite successful in refuting step (ii) in the Argument from the Poverty of the Stimulus, but it does not really explain where the preferences of children come from. Actually it only explains that these preferences come from child-directed input provided by caregivers. Thus the next question is: where do the caregivers get their preferences from? From *their* caregivers -- ad infinitum? It is exactly the goal of generative grammar to try to answer these questions. But as we have shown in this paper, these answers are motivated by an argument that does not hold. Thus our work should be seen as (1) a refutation of this argument (of the Poverty of the Stimulus) and (2) an alternative approach that can model all the hard phenomena on the basis of just one principle (the best-ranked derivation). The question where the preferences may eventually come from, should be answered within the field of language evolution.

While our TSG could successfully learn a number of linguistic phenomena, it still has shortcomings. We already explained that we have only tested on part of speech strings. While this is not essentially different from how the nativist approach defines their constraints (i.e. on categories and functions of words, not on specific words themselves), we believe that any final model should be tested on word strings. Moreover, we have tested only on English. There is a major question how our approach performs on other languages, for example, with rich morphology.

So far, our model only ranks alternative sentences (for a certain phenomenon). Ideally, we would want to test a system that produces for a given meaning to be conveyed the various possible sentences ordered in terms of their rankings, from which the top-ranked sentence is taken. In the absence of a semantic component in our model, we could only test the already given alternative sentences and assess whether our model could predict the correct one.

Despite these problems, our main result is that with just a tiny fraction of a child's input the correct sentence can be predicted by an unsupervised TSG for virtually all phenomena related to wh-questions as well as for a number of other phenomena that even fall out of the scope of the traditional generativist account.

Finally it should be noted that our result is not in contrast with all generativist work. For example, in Hauser et al. (2002), it was proposed that the core language faculty comprises just recursive tree structure and nothing else. The work presented in this paper may be the first to show that one general grammar induction algorithm makes language learning possible for a much wider set of phenomena than has previously been endeavored.

If empiricist models want to compete with generativist models, they should compete in the same arena, with the same phenomena.

References

D. Adger, 2003. *Core syntax: A minimalist approach*. Oxford University Press, 2003.

B. Ambridge and E. Lieven, 2011). *Child Language Acquisition. Contrasting Theoretical Approaches*. Cambridge University Press.

M. Bansal and D. Klein, 2011. The Surprising Variance in Shortest-Derivation Parsing, *Proceedings ACL-HLT 2011*.

C. Bannard, E. Lieven and M. Tomasello, 2009. Modeling Children's Early Grammatical Knowledge, *Proceedings of the National Academy of Sciences*, 106, 17284-89.

R. Bod, R. Scha and K. Sima'an (eds.), 2003. *Data-Oriented Parsing*, CSLI Publications/University of Chicago Press.

R. Bod, 2006. An all-subtrees approach to unsupervised parsing. *Proceedings ACL-COLING*.

R. Bod, 2009. From Exemplar to Grammar: A Probabilistic Analogy-based Model of Language Learning. *Cognitive Science*, 33(5), 752-793.

R. Borsley, 2004. *Syntactic Theory: A Unified Approach*, Oxford University Press.

A. Clark and R. Eyraud, 2006. Learning Auxiliary Fronting with Grammatical Inference. *Proceedings CONLL 2006*.

A. Clark and S. Lappin, 2011. *Linguistic Nativism and the Poverty of the Stimulus*, Wiley-Blackwell.

T. Cohn, P. Blunsom, and S. Goldwater, 2010. Inducing Tree-Substitution Grammars, *Journal of Machine Learning Research*, JMLR 11, 3053-3096.

S. Crain, 1991. Language acquisition in the absence of experience. *Behavorial and Brain Sciences*, 14, 597-612.

S. Crain and R. Thornton. Acquisition of syntax and semantics, 2006. In M. Traxler and M. Gernsbacher, editors, *Handbook of Psycholinguistics*. Elsevier.

S. Foraker, T. Regier, N. Khetarpal, A. Perfors, and J. Tenenbaum, 2009. Indirect Evidence and the Poverty of the Stimulus: The Case of Anaphoric One. *Cognitive Science*, 33, 287-300.

J. Goodman, 2003. Efficient parsing of DOP with PCFG-reductions. In R. Bod, R. Scha & K. Sima'an (Eds.), *Data-oriented parsing*, 125–146. CSLI Pubs.

M. Hauser, N. Chomsky and T. Fitch, 2002. The faculty of language: What is it, who has it, and how did it evolve? *Science*, 298, 1569–1579.

L . Huang and D. Chiang, 2005. Better k-best parsing. In *Proceedings IWPT 2005*, pp. 53–64.

X. Kam, L. Stoyneshka, L. Tornyova, J. Fodor and W. Sakas, 2008. Bigrams and the Richness of the Stimulus. *Cognitive Science*, *32*, 771-787.

D. Klein and C. Manning, 2005 Natural language grammar induction with a generative constituent-context model. *Pattern Recognition*, 38, 1407–1419.

J. Lidz, S. Waxman and J. Freedman, 2003. What infants know about syntax but couldn't have learned: experimental evidence for syntactic structure at 18 months. *Cognition*, 89, B65–B73

B. MacWhinney, 2000. *The CHILDES project: Tools for analyzing talk*. Mawah, NJ: Erlbaum

B. MacWhinney, 2004. A multiple process solution to the logical problem of language acquisition. *Journal of Child Language*, 3, 883- 914.

T. O'Donnell, N. Goodman, and J. Tenenbaum, 2009. Fragment grammar: Exploring reuse in hierarchical generative processes. *Technical Report MIT-CSAIL-TR-2009-013*, MIT.

M. Post and D. Gildea, 2009. Bayesian learning of a tree substitution grammar. In *Proceedings of the ACL-IJCNLP 2009*.

G. Pullum and B. Scholz, 2002. Empirical assessment of stimulus povery arguments. *The Linguist Review, 19(2002)*, 9-50.

F. Reali and M. Christiansen, 2005. Uncovering the richness of the stimulus: structure dependence and indirect statistical evidence. *Cognitive Science*, *29*, 1007-1028.

J. Ross, 1967. *Constraints on variables in syntax*. PhD thesis, Massachusetts Institute of Technology.

C. Teichmann, 2011. Reducing the size of the representation for the uDOP-estimate. *Proceedings EMNLP 2011*.

H. Waterfall, B. Sandbank, L. Onnis, and S. Edelman, 2010. An empirical generative framework for computational modeling of language acquisition. *Journal of Child Language*, 37, 671-703.

A. Zollmann and K. Sima'an. 2005. A Consistent and Efficient Estimator for Data-Oriented Parsing. In *Journal of Automata, Languages and Combinatorics*, 10 (2005), 367-388.

Probabilistic Models of Grammar Acquisition

Mark Steedman

University of Edinburgh
steedman@inf.ed.ac.uk

The most convincing models of human grammar acquisition to date are supervised, in the sense that they learn from pairs of strings and meaning representations (Siskind, 1996; Villavicencio, 2002; Villavicencio, 2011; Buttery, 2004; Buttery, 2006; Kwiatkowski et al., 2012). Although the principles by which such models learn are quite general, the datasets they have been applied to have unavoidably been somewhat target-language-specific, and are also limited to discourse-external world-state-related content, contrary to the observations of (Tomasello, 2001) concerning the central role of common ground and grounding in interpersonal interaction.

I'll review the state of the art in the light of these limitations on the datasets, and try to make some suggestions about how we might obtain more realistic and challenging artificial and natural datasets using both automatic and human labeling methods.

References

Paula Buttery. 2004. A quantitative evaluation of naturalistic models of language acquisition: the efficiency of the Triggering Learning Algorithm compared to a Categorial Grammar Learner. In *Proceedings of the First Workshop on Psycho-computational Models of Human Language Acquisition*, pages 1–6.

Paula J. Buttery. 2006. Computational models for first language acquisition. Technical Report UCAM-CL-TR-675, University of Cambridge, Computer Laboratory.

Tom Kwiatkowski, Sharon Goldwater, Luke Zettelmoyer, and Mark Steedman. 2012. A probabilistic model of syntactic and semantic acquisition from child-directed utterances and their meanings. In *Proceedings of the 13th Conference of the European Chapter of the Association for Computational Linguistics*.

Jeffery Mark Siskind. 1996. A computational study of cross-situational techniques for learning word-to-meaning mappings. *Cognition*, 61:39–91.

Michael Tomasello. 2001. Perceiving intentions and learning words in the second year of life. In Melissa Bowerman and Stephen Levinson, editors, *Language Acquisition and Conceptual Development*, pages 132–158. Cambridge University Press, Cambridge.

Aline Villavicencio. 2002. The acquisition of a unification-based generalised categorial grammar. Technical Report UCAM-CL-TR-533, University of Cambridge,Computer Laboratory.

Aline Villavicencio. 2011. Language acquisition with a unification-based grammar. In R. Borsley e K. Borjars, editor, *Non-transformational Syntax*. Blackwell.

A Morphologically Annotated Hebrew CHILDES Corpus

Aviad Albert
Linguistics
Tel Aviv Uni.
Israel

Brian MacWhinney
Psychology
Carnegie Mellon Uni.
USA

Bracha Nir
Communication Sciences
Uni. of Haifa
Israel

Shuly Wintner
Computer Science
Uni. of Haifa
Israel

Abstract We present a corpus of transcribed spoken Hebrew that reflects spoken interactions between children and adults. The corpus is an integral part of the CHILDES database, which distributes similar corpora for over 25 languages. We introduce a dedicated transcription scheme for the spoken Hebrew data that is sensitive to both the phonology and the standard orthography of the language. We also introduce a morphological analyzer that was specifically developed for this corpus. The analyzer adequately covers the entire corpus, producing detailed correct analyses for all tokens. Evaluation on a new corpus reveals high coverage as well. Finally, we describe a morphological disambiguation module that selects the correct analysis of each token in context. The result is a high-quality morphologically-annotated CHILDES corpus of Hebrew, along with a set of tools that can be applied to new corpora.

CHILDES We present a corpus of transcribed spoken Hebrew that forms an integral part of a comprehensive data system that has been developed to suit the specific needs and interests of child language researchers: CHILDES (MacWhinney, 2000). CHILDES is a system of programs and codes designed to facilitate the process of free speech analysis. It involves three integrated components: 1. *CHAT*, a system for discourse notation and coding, designed to accommodate a large variety of analyses, while still permitting a barebones form of transcription; 2. *CLAN*, a set of computer programs; and 3. A large, internationally recognized database of language transcripts formatted in CHAT. These include child-caretaker interactions from normally-developing children, children with language disorders, adults with aphasia, learners of second languages, and bilinguals who have been exposed to language in early childhood. Researchers can directly test a vast range of empirical hypotheses against data from nearly a hundred major research projects. While about half of the CHILDES corpus consists of English data, there is also a significant body of transcripts in 25 other languages.

Corpus We focus on the Hebrew section of CHILDES, consisting of two corpora: the Berman longitudinal corpus, with data from four children between the ages of 1;06 and 3;05 (Berman and Weissenborn, 1991), and the Ravid longitudinal corpus, with data from two siblings between the ages of 0;09 to around 6 years of age. The corpora consist of 110,819 utterances comprising of 417,938 word-tokens (13,828 word-types).

Transcription The Hebrew data are transcribed with a Latin-based phonemic transcription (Nir et al., 2010). We use a set of monoglyph Unicode characters (mostly in line with standard IPA conventions) that has already been applied for other complex scripts. In contrast to previous transcription methods, the current transcription reflects phonemic, orthographic and prosodic features. The advantages of our approach in reducing ambiguity are:

- Unlike the standard script, our phonemic transcriptions includes the five vowels of Modern Hebrew, and prosodic information on primary stress location, thereby yielding fewer ambiguities that stem from homographs.
- At the same time, we retain valuable phonemic and phonetic distinctions that are standard in the orthography but are no longer distinct in Modern Hebrew speech (e.g., *t*/*ṭ*, *k*/*q*, *ʔ*/*ʕ*).
- We separate and mark prefix particles, making it easier to recognize them as separate morphemes, which never participate in homographs.

Our transcription thus conforms to the three major goals which the CHAT format is designed to achieve (MacWhinney, 1996): systematicity and clarity, human and computerized readability, and ease of data entry.

Morphological Analysis CLAN includes a language for expressing morphological grammars, implemented as a system, *MOR*, for the construction of morphological analyzers. A MOR grammar consists of three components: a set of *lexicons* specifying lexical entries (base lexemes) and lists of affixes; a set of rules that govern allomorphic changes in the stems of lexical entries (*A-rules*); and a set of rules that govern linear affixation processes by concatenation (*C-rules*).

Different languages vary in their requirements and their need to utilize these MOR devices. The Hebrew MOR extensively uses all of them in order to account for vocalic and consonantal changes of the stem allomorphs (handled within the A-Rules), and the proper affixation possibilities (via the C-rules and affix lists).

The *lexicon* includes over 5,800 entries, in 16 part-of-speech (POS) categories. Lexically-specified information includes root and pattern (for verbs mainly), gender (for nouns), plural suffix (for nouns), and other information that cannot be deduced from the form of the word. Over 1,000 A-rules describe various allomorphs of morphological paradigms, listing their morphological and morphosyntactic features, including number, gender, person, nominal status, tense, etc. Lexical entries then instantiate the paradigms described by the rules, thereby generating specific allomorphs. These, in turn, can combine with affixes via over 100 C-rules that govern the morphological alternations involved in affixation.

Results and Evaluation The corpora include over 400,000 word tokens (about 14,000 types). More than 27,000 different morphological analyses are produced for the tokens observed in the corpus; however, we estimate that the application of the morphological rules to our lexicon would result in hundreds of thousands of forms, so that the coverage of the MOR grammar is substantially wider. The grammar fully covers our current corpus. Figure 1 depicts a small fragment of a morphologically-annotated corpus.

To evaluate the coverage of the grammar, we applied it to a new corpus that is currently being transcribed. Of the 10,070 tokens in this corpus, 176 (1.75%) do not obtain an analysis (77 of the 1431 types, 5.3%). While some analyses may be wrong, we believe that most of them are valid, and that the gaps can be attributed mostly to missing lexical entries and inconsistent transcription.

As another evaluation method, we developed a program that converts the transcription we use to the standard Hebrew script. We then submit the Hebrew forms to the MILA morphological analyzer (Itai and Wintner, 2008), and compare the results. The mismatch rate is 11%. While few mismatches indeed indicate errors in the MOR grammar, many are attributable to problems with the MILA analyzer or the conversion and comparison script.

Morphological Disambiguation The MOR grammar associates each surface form with *all* its possible analyses, independently of the context. This results in morphological ambiguity. The level of ambiguity is much lower than that of the standard Hebrew script, especially due to the vocalic information encoded in the transcription, but several forms are still ambiguous. These include frequent words that can function both as nouns, adjectives or adverbs and as communicators (e.g., *yōfi* "beauty/great!", *ṭov* "good/OK"); verbs whose tense is ambiguous (e.g., *baʔ* "come" can be either present or past); etc.

We manually disambiguated 18 of the 304 files in the corpus, and used them to train a POS tagger with tools that are embedded in CLAN (*POSTRAIN* and *POST*). We then automatically disambiguated the remaining files. Preliminary evaluation shows 80% accuracy on ambiguous tokens.

Future Plans Our ultimate plan is to add syntactic annotation to the transcripts. We have devised a syntactic annotation scheme, akin to the existing scheme used for the English section of CHILDES (Sagae et al., 2010), but with special consideration for Hebrew constructions that are common in the corpora. We have recently begun to annotate the corpora according to this scheme.

Acknowledgments This research was supported by Grant No. 2007241 from the United States-Israel Binational Science Foundation (BSF). We are grateful to Arnon Lazerson for developing the conversion script, and to Shai Gretz for helping with the manual annotation.

```
@Begin
@Languages:	heb
@Participants:	CHI Sivan Target_Child, CHA Asaf Target_Child, MOT Dorit_Ravid Mother
@ID:	heb|ravid|CHI|2;2.19|||Target_Child||
@ID:	heb|ravid|CHA|1;1.03|||Target_Child||
@ID:	heb|ravid|MOT||||Mother||
@ID:	heb|ravid|FAT||||Father||
@Date:	03-SEP-1980
@Situation:	Child plays with parents.
@Comment:	one in series of 20 such recordings.
@Comment:	Number of utterances CHI is 93, CHA is 13, total is 264
*CHI:	ma ze ?
%mor:	que|ma=what
	pro:dem|ze&pers:3&gen:ms&num:sg=it/this ?
*MOT:	nu ma ze Siwān ?
%mor:	co|nu=hurry_up
	que|ma=what
	pro:dem|ze&pers:3&gen:ms&num:sg=it/this
	n:prop|Siwān ?
*CHI:	baqbūq .
%mor:	n|baqbūq&gen:ms&num:sg&stat:unsp .
*MOT:	bōʔi, bōʔi rēgaʕ hēna, bōʔi rēgaʕ hēna .
%mor:	v|baʔ&root:bwʔ&ptn:qal&form:imp&pers:2&gen:fm&num:sg-i=come
	v|baʔ&root:bwʔ&ptn:qal&form:imp&pers:2&gen:fm&num:sg-i=come
	n|rēgaʕ&root:rgʕ&ptn:qetel&gen:ms&num:sg&stat:unsp=moment
	adv|hēna=here/to_here
	v|baʔ&root:bwʔ&ptn:qal&form:imp&pers:2&gen:fm&num:sg-i=come
	n|rēgaʕ&root:rgʕ&ptn:qetel&gen:ms&num:sg&stat:unsp=moment
	adv|hēna=here/to_here .
```

Figure 1: A fragment of the annotated corpus

References

Ruth A. Berman and Jürgen Weissenborn. Acquisition of word order: A crosslinguistic study. Final Report. German-Israel Foundation for Research and Development (GIF), 1991.

Alon Itai and Shuly Wintner. Language resources for Hebrew. *Language Resources and Evaluation*, 42 (1):75–98, March 2008.

Brian MacWhinney. The CHILDES system. *American Journal of Speech Language Pathology*, 5:5–14, 1996.

Brian MacWhinney. *The CHILDES Project: Tools for Analyzing Talk*. Lawrence Erlbaum Associates, Mahwah, NJ, third edition, 2000.

Bracha Nir, Brian MacWhinney, and Shuly Wintner. A morphologically-analyzed CHILDES corpus of Hebrew. In *Proceedings of the Seventh conference on International Language Resources and Evaluation (LREC'10)*, pages 1487–1490, Valletta, Malta, May 2010. European Language Resources Association (ELRA). ISBN 2-9517408-6-7.

Kenji Sagae, Eric Davis, Alon Lavie, Brian MacWhinney, and Shuly Wintner. Morphosyntactic annotation of CHILDES transcripts. *Journal of Child Language*, 37(3):705–729, 2010. doi: 10.1017/S0305000909990407. URL `http://journals.cambridge.org/article_S0305000909990407`.

An annotated English child language database

Aline Villavicencio[♣♠], Beracah Yankama[♠], Rodrigo Wilkens[♣],
Marco A. P. Idiart[♣], Robert Berwick[♠]

[♣]Federal University of Rio Grande do Sul (Brazil)
[♠]MIT (USA)

alinev@gmail.com, beracah@mit.edu, rswilkens@gmail.com, marco.idiart@gmail.com, berwick@csail.mit.edu

1 Introduction

The use of large-scale naturalistic data has been opening up new investigative possibilities for language acquisition studies, providing a basis for empirical predictions and for evaluations of alternative acquisition hypotheses. One widely used resource is CHILDES (MacWhinney, 1995) with transcriptions for over 25 languages of interactions involving children, with the English corpora available in raw, part-of-speech tagged, lemmatized and parsed formats (Sagae et al., 2010; Buttery and Korhonen, 2005). With a recent increase in the availability of lexical and psycholinguistic resources and robust natural language processing tools, it is now possible to further enrich child-language corpora with additional sources of information.

In this paper we describe the English CHILDES Verb Database (ECVD), which extends the original lexical and syntactic annotation of verbs in CHILDES with information about frequency, grammatical relations, semantic classes, and other psycholinguistic and statistical information. In addition, these corpora are organized in a searchable database that allows the retrieval of data according to complex queries that combine different sources of information. This database is also modular and can be straightforwardly extended with additional annotation levels. In what follows, we discuss the tools and resources used for the annotation (§2), and conclude with a discussion of the implications of this initial work along with directions for future research (§3).

2 Linguistic and Statistical Properties

The English CHILDES Verb Database contains information about the English corpora in CHILDES parsed using three different pipelines: (1) MEGRASP; (2) RASP; and (3) the CHILDES Treebank. In the first, made available as part of the CHILDES distribution[1], the corpora are POS tagged (in %mor), and parsed using MEGRASP (Sagae et al., 2010) which provides information about dependency parses and grammatical relations (in %gra):[2]

*MOT:	I said (.) Adam you could have a banana and offer Robin and Ursula one (.)would you ?
%mor:	pro|I v|say&PAST n:prop|Adam pro|you aux|could v|have det|a n|banana ...
%gra:	1|2|SUBJ 2|6|CJCT 3|2|OBJ 4|6|SUBJ 5|6|AUX 6|9|COORD 7|8|DET 8|6|OBJ ...

In the second pipeline, the RASP system (Briscoe et al., 2006) is used for tokenisation, tagging, lemmatization and parsing of the input sentences, outputting syntactic trees (in %ST) and grammatical relations (%GR).[3] In both examples each GR denotes a relation, along with its head and dependent:

*MOT:	oh no # he didn't say anything about window .
%ST:	(T Oh:1 no:2 ,:3 (S he:4 (VP do+ed:5 not+:6 say:7 anything:8 (PP about:9 (N1 window:10)))) .:11)
%GR:	(|ncsubj| |say:7_VV0| |he:4_PPHS1| _) (|aux| |say:7_VV0| |do+ed:5_VDD|) (|ncmod| _ |say:7_VV0| |not+:6_XX|) (|iobj| |say:7_VV0| |about:9_II|) (|dobj| |say:7_VV0| |anything:8_PN1|) (|dobj| |about:9_II| |window:10_NN1|)

The third focuses on the Adam corpus from the Brown data set (Brown, 1973) and uses the Charniak parser with Penn Treebank style part of speech tags and output, followed by hand-curation, as described by Pearl and Sprouse (2012):

(S1 (SBARQ (WHNP (WP who)) (SQ (VP (COP is) (NP (NN that)))) (. ?)))

[1]http://childes.psy.cmu.edu/

[2]In an evaluation MEGRASP produced correct dependency relations for 96% of the relations in the gold standard, with the dependency relations being labelled with the correct GR 94% of the time.

[3]The data was kindly provided by P. Buttery and A. Korhonen and generated as described in (Buttery and Korhonen, 2005).

The use of annotations from multiple parsers enables the combination of the complementary strengths of each in terms of coverage and accuracy, similar to inter-annotator agreement approaches. These differences are also useful for optimizing search patterns in terms of the source which produces the best accuracy for a particular case. Information about corpora sizes and the annotated portions for each of the parsers is displayed in table 1.

Information	Sentences
Total Raw	4.84 million
MEGRASP & RASP Raw	2.5 million
MEGRASP Parsed	109,629
RASP Parsed	2.21 million
CHILDES Treebank	26,280
MEGRASP & RASP Parsed	98,456

Table 1: Parsed Sentences

The verbs in each sentence are also annotated with information about shared patterns of meaning and syntactic behavior from 190 fine-grained subclasses that cover 3,100 verb types (Levin, 1993). This annotation allows searches defined in terms of verb classes, and include all sentences that contain verbs that belong to a given class. For instance, searching for verbs of running would return sentences containing not only *run* but also related verbs like *slide, roll* and *stroll*.

Additional annotation of properties linked to language use and recognition include extrinsic factors such as word frequency and intrinsic factors such as the length of a word in terms of syllables; age of acquisition; imageability; and familiarity. Some of this annotation is obtained from the MRC Psycholinguistic Database (Coltheart, 1981) which contains 150,837 entries with information about 26 properties, although not all properties are available for every word (e.g. IMAG is only available for 9,240 words).

For enabling complex search functionalities that potentially combine information from several sources, the annotated sentences were organized in a database, and Tables 2 and 3 list some of the available annotations. Given the focus on verbs, for search efficiency each sentence is indexed according to the verbs it contains. In addition, verbs and nouns are further annotated with information shown in table 3 whenever it is available in the existing resources.

These levels of annotation allow for complex searches involving for example, a combination of information about a verb's lemma, target grammatical relations, and occurrence of Levin's classes in the corpora.

Not all sentences have been successfully analyzed, and the comments field contains information about the missing annotations and cases of near perfect matches that arise from the parsers using different heuristics for e.g. non-words, metacharacters and punctuation. These required more complex matching procedures for identifying the corresponding cases in the annotations of the parsers.

Fields
Sentence ID
Corpus
Speaker
File
Raw sentence
MOR and POST tags
MEGRASP dep. and GRs
RASP syntactic tree
RASP dep. and GRs
Comments

Table 2: Information about Sentences

Fields
Word ID
Sentence ID
Levin's classes
Age of acquisition
Familiarity
Concreteness
Frequency
Imageability
Number of syllables

Table 3: Information about Words

3 Conclusions and future work

This paper describes the construction of the English CHILDES Verb Database. It combines information from different parsing systems to capitalize on their complementary recall and precision strengths and ensure the accuracy of the searches. It also includes information about Levin's classes for verbs, and some psycholinguistic information for some of the words, like age of acquisition, familiarity and imageability. The result is a large-scale integrated resource that allows complex searches involving different annotation levels. This database can be used to inform analysis, for instance, about the complexity of the language employed with and by a child as her age increases, that can shed some light on discussions about the poverty of the stimulus. This is an ongoing project to make the annotated data available to the research community in a user-friendly interface that allows complex patterns to be specified in a simple way.

Acknowledgements

This research was partly supported by CNPq Projects 551964/2011-1, 202007/2010-3,

305256/2008-4 and 309569/2009-5.

References

E. Briscoe, J. Carroll, and R. Watson. 2006. The second release of the rasp system. In *Proceedings of the COLING/ACL 2006 Interactive Presentation Sessions*, Sydney, Australia.

R. Brown. 1973. *A first language: The early stages*. Harvard University Press, Cambridge, Massachusetts.

P. Buttery and A. Korhonen. 2005. Large-scale analysis of verb subcategorization differences between child directed speech and adult speech. In *Proceedings of the Interdisciplinary Workshop on the Identification and Representation of Verb Features and Verb Classes*.

M. Coltheart. 1981. The MRC psycholinguistic database. *Quarterly Journal of Experimental Psychology*, 33A:497–505.

B. Levin. 1993. *English verb classes and alternations - a preliminary investigation*. The University of Chicago Press.

B. MacWhinney. 1995. *The CHILDES project: tools for analyzing talk*. Hillsdale, NJ: Lawrence Erlbaum Associates, second edition.

L. Pearl and J. Sprouse, 2012. *Experimental Syntax and Islands Effects*, chapter Computational Models of Acquisition for Islands. Cambridge University Press.

K. Sagae, E. Davis, A. Lavie, B. MacWhinney, and S. Wintner. 2010. Morphosyntactic annotation of CHILDES transcripts. *Journal of Child Language*, 37(03):705–729.

Searching the Annotated Portuguese Childes Corpora

Rodrigo Wilkens
Institute of Informatics
Federal University of Rio Grande do Sul
Brazil
rswilkens@inf.ufrgs.br

1 Introduction

Annotated corpora of child language data are valuable resources for language acquisition studies, for instance, providing the basis for developmental comparisons and evaluation of different hypotheses. For computational investigations annotated corpora can serve as an approximation to the linguistic environment to which a child is exposed, as discussed by Wintner (2010).

Recently there has been a growing number of initiatives for annotating children's data for a number of languages, with for instance, part-of-speech (PoS) and syntactic information (Sagae et al., 2010; Buttery and Korhonen, 2007; Yang, 2010) and some of these are available as part of CHILDES (MacWhinney, 2000). For resource rich languages like English these annotations can be further extended with detailed information, for instance, from WordNet (Fellbaum, 1998) about synonymy, from the MRC Psycholinguistic Database (Coltheart, 1981) about age of acquisition, imagery, concreteness and familiarity among others. However, for many other languages one of the challenges is in annotating corpora in a context where resources and tools are less abundant and many are still under development.

In this paper we describe one such initiative, for annotating the raw Portuguese corpora available in the CHILDES database with (psycho)linguistic and distributional information (§2) . It also describes a modular searching environment for these corpora that allows complex and flexible searches that combine different levels of annotation, and that can be easily extended (§3). We finish with some conclusions and future work.

2 Resource Description

The Portuguese, CHILDES contains 3 corpora:

- Batoréo (Batoreo, 2000) with 60 narratives, 30 from adults and 30 from children, about two stories
- Porto Alegre (Guimarães, 1994; Guimarães, 1995) with data from 5 to 9 year old children, collected both cross-sectionally and longitudinally and
- Florianópolis with the longitudinal data for one Brazilian child: 5530 utterances in broad phonetic transcription.

The total number of sentences and words per age in these corpora is shown in Table 1

Table 1: Frequency of words and sentences per age in the Portuguese corpora

Age	words	sentences
0	0	0
1	7k	2k
2	8k	1k
3	0	0
4	1k	61
5	38k	1k
6	47k	1k
7	56k	1k
8	56k	1k

In order to annotate the transcribed sentences in the CHILDES Portuguese corpora we used the PALAVRAS parser[1] (Bick, 2000). It is a statistical robust Portuguese parser, which always return

[1]Tagset avaliable at http://beta.visl.sdu.dk/visl/pt/info/symbolset-manual.html.

at least one analysis even for incomplete or ungrammatical sentences. This parser has a high accuracy: 99% for part-of-speech and 96-97%. The parser also has a named entity recognizer (Bick, 2003) and provides some semantic information for nouns, verbs and adjectives (e.g. organization, date, place, etc). The annotations process consisted of the following steps:

1. automatic pre-processing for dealing with incomplete words and removing transcription notes;

2. tagging and parsing with PALAVRAS parser;

3. annotation of verbs and nouns with psycholinguistic information like age of acquisition and concreteness from (Cameirao and Vicente, 2010).

For enabling age related analysis, the sentences were subsequently divided according to the child's age reported in each corpus, and annotated with frequency information collected considering separately each type of annotation per age.

3 System Description

In order to allow complex searches that combine information from different levels of annotation for each age, the sentences were organized in a database, structured as in Tables 2 and 3, respectively presenting the structure of words and sentences).

Table 2: Information about Words

Word
age of acquisition
part-of-speech
corpus frequency
frequency by age
adult frequency

Table 3: Information about Sentences

Sentence
children gender
PoS tags
dependency tree
semantic tags

Using a web environment, a user can choose any combination of fields in the database to perform a query. It is possible to examine, for instance, the usage of a particular word and its evolution according to grammatical class per age.

The environment provides two modes for queries: an expert mode, where database queries can be dynamically specified selecting the relevant fields, and a guided mode which contains predefined query components and a set of filters that users can combine in the queries. The results are available both as a file containing the relevant annotated sentences for further processing, or in a graphical form. The latter shows a chart of frequency per age, which can be displayed in terms of absolute or relative values.

The guided mode provides an iterative way for query construction where the user selects a relevant field (e.g. age of acquisition) at a time and adds it to the query until all desired fields have been added, when the resulting query is saved. The user can repeat this process to create combined queries and at the end of the process can chose the form for outputting the result (graphic or file).

4 Conclusion

This paper describes the (psycho)linguistic and distributional annotation of the Portuguese corpora in CHILDES, and presents an environment for searching them. This environment allows complex searches combining multiple levels of annotation to be created even by non-expert users. Therefore this initiative not only produced an integrated and rich annotation schema so far lacking for these corpora, but also provided a modular environment for structuring and searching them through a more user friendly interface. As next steps we foresee the extension of the annotation using other resources. We also plan to add corpora for other languages to the environment, such as English and Spanish.

Acknowledgements

This research was partly supported by CNPq Projects 551964/2011-1 and 478222/2011-4.

References

Batoréo, H. 2000. *Expressão do Espaço no Português Europeu. Contributo Psicolinguístico para o Estudo da Linguagem e Cognição.* PhD Dissertation, Fundação Calouste Gulbenkian e Fundação para a Ciência e a Tecnologia, Ministério da Ciência e da Tecnologia, Lisboa

Bick, E. 2000. *The Parsing System Palavras. Automatic Grammatical Analysis of Portuguese in a Constraint Grammar Framework.* [S.l.]: University of Arhus.

Bick, E. 2003. *Multi-level NER for Portuguese in a CG framework.* Proceedings of the Computational Processing of the Portuguese Language.

Briscoe, E., Carroll, J., and Watson, R. 2006. *The second release of the rasp system.* COLING/ACL 2006 Interactive Presentation Sessions, Sydney, Australia.

Buttery, P., Korhonen, A. 2007. *I will shoot your shopping down and you can shoot all my tins– Automatic Lexical Acquisition from the CHILDES Database.* Proceedings of the Workshop on Cognitive Aspects of Computational Language Acquisition. Association for Computational Linguistics.

Cameirao, M.L. and Vicente, S.G. 2010. *Age-of-acquisition norms for a set of 1,749 portuguese words.* Behavior research methods 42, Springer.

Coltheart, M. 1981. The MRC psycholinguistic database. *Quarterly Journal of Experimental Psychology*, 33A:497–505.

Fellbaum, C. 1998. *WordNet An Electronic Lexical Database.*. The MIT Press, Cambridge, MA ; London.

Guimarães, A. M. 1994. *Desenvolvimento da linguagem da criança na fase deletramento.* Cadernos de Estudos Linguísticos, 26, 103-110

Guimarães, A. M. 1994. *The use of the CHILDES database for Brazilian Portuguese.* I. H. Faria & M. J. Freitas (Eds.), Studies on the acquisition of Portuguese. Lisbon: Colibri

MacWhinney, B. 2000. *The CHILDES project: tools for analyzing talk.* Lawrence Erlbaum Associates, second edition.

Sagae, K., Davis, E., Lavie, A., MacWhinney, B. and Wintner, S. 2010. *Morphosyntactic annotation of CHILDES transcripts.* Journal of Child Language.

Wintner, S. 2010. *Computational Models of Language Acquisition.* CICLing'10.

Charles, Yang 2010. *Three factors in language variation.* Lingua.

Web Services for Bayesian Learning

Muntsa Padró
Universitat Pompeu Fabra
Barcelona, Spain
muntsa.padro@upf.edu

Núria Bel
Universitat Pompeu Fabra
Barcelona, Spain
nuria.bel@upf.edu

Abstract

In this demonstration we present our web services to perform Bayesian learning for classification tasks.

1 Introduction

The Bayesian framework for probabilistic inference has been proposed (for instance, Griffiths et al., 2008 and a survey in Chater and Manning, 2006 for language related topics) as a general approach to understanding how problems of induction can be solved given only the sparse and noisy data that humans observe. In particular, how human acquire words if the available data severely limit the possibility of making inferences. Bayesian framework has been proposed as way to introduce a priori knowledge to guide the inference process. In particular for Lexical Acquisition, Xu and Tenembaum (2007) proposed that given a hypothesis space (all what a word can be, according to a set of existing classes) and one or more examples of a new word, the learner evaluates all hypotheses for candidate word classes by computing their posterior probabilities, proportional to the product of prior probabilities and likelihood. The prior probabilities are the learner's beliefs about which hypotheses are more or less plausible. The likelihood reflects the learner's expectations about which examples are likely to be observed given a particular hypothesis about a word class. And the decision on new words is determined by averaging the predictions of all hypothesis weighted by their posterior probabilities.

The hypothesis behind is that natural language characteristics, such as the Zipfian distribution of words (Zipf, 1935) and considerations as the classic argument on sparse data (Chomsky, 1980), make it necessary to postulate that the learning of words must be guided by the knowledge of the lexical system itself, information about abstracted, not directly observable categories (Goldberg, 2006; Bybee, 1998).

In order to test this hypothesis we developed a series of tools for the task of noun classification into lexical semantic classes (such as EVENT, HUMAN, LOCATION, etc.). The tools perform Bayesian parameter estimation where prior knowledge is included into the parameters as virtual evidence (following Griffiths et al. 2008) and a Naive Bayes based classification. Our assumption is that, if introducing prior knowledge improves the classification results, it may give some insights about the way humans learn lexical classes.

The developed tools have been deployed as web services (following web-based architecture of the PANACEA project[1]) in order to make them easily available to the community. They can be used in the task just mentioned but also in other tasks that may profit from a Bayesian approach.

2 Web Services for Bayesian modeling

In this demonstration, we present two web services that can be used for Bayesian inference of parameters and classification with the aim that they may be useful to other researchers willing to use Bayesian methods in their research.

2.1 Naive Bayes Classifier

A first web service performs a traditional Naive Bayes classification. The input is the observed data from a given instance encoded as cue vectors, this is, the number of times we have seen each cue in the context of the studied instance. Then, the web service computes how likely is that this instance belongs to a particular class. The input needed by the classifier is the set of probabilities of seeing each cue given each class $P(cue_i|k)$. Those parameters should have

[1] http://panacea-lr.eu/

been previously induced (using Maximum Likelihood Estimation (MLE), a Bayesian approach, etc.).

The classifier web service reads those probabilities from a coma separated file and the cue vectors of the instances we want to classify in Weka format (Quinlan, 1993). In our implementation, we work with binary classification, i.e. we want to decide whether the noun belongs or does not belong to a given class. Thus, the service returns the most likely class for each instance given the parameters and a score for this classification (i.e. how different was the probability of being and not being a member of the class).

2.2 Bayesian Estimation of Probabilities

A second web service performs parameter inference for the Naive Bayes classifier using Bayesian methods.

Bayesian methods (Griffiths et al., 2008; Mackay, 2003) are a formal framework to introduce prior knowledge when estimating the parameters (probabilities) of a given system. The main difference between those methods and MLE is that the latter use only data to estimate parameters, while the former use both data and prior knowledge.

An example of Bayesian learning is determining the probability of a coin producing heads in a short throw series. A MLE approach will determine this probability as $p(head) \approx \frac{N_{heads}}{N}$. Thus, after observing a sequence of 5 heads in a row, MLE would assess that the probability of the coin producing heads is 1. Nevertheless, because of our knowledge, we would rather say that a tail is more than possible, and that the coin probability can still be close to 0.5. Bayesian models allow us to formally introduce this knowledge when estimating the probabilities.

In the case of Naive Bayes classification using cue vectors, we need to estimate $P(cue_i|k)$ for each cue and k (for binary classification this would be k=1 for being a member of the class and k=0 for not being a member of the class).

Bayesian modelling computes these parameters approximating them by their Maximum a Posteriori (MAP) estimator. The canonical approach introduces the prior probabilities as a Beta distribution, and leads to the following MAP estimator (see Griffiths et al. (2008) and Mackay (2003) for details):

$$MAP = \hat{P}(cue_i|k) = \frac{N^i_{yes}(k) + V^i_{yes}(k)}{N^i_{yes}(k) + V^i_{yes}(k) + N^i_{no}(k) + V^i_{no}(k)}$$

Where $N^i_{yes}(k)$ and $N^i_{no}(k)$ are the observed occurrences in real data ($N^i_{yes}(k)$ is the number of times we have seen cue_i with class k and $N^i_{no}(k)$ is the number of times we have not seen it, and $V^i_{yes}(k)$ and $V^i_{no}(k)$ represent what is called *virtual data*, this is, the data we expect to observe a priori. Thus, it can be seen from the MAP estimator that Bayesian inference allows us to add virtual data to actual evidence.

The web service we want to show in this demonstration implements the estimation of $P(cue_i|k)$ combining the data and the priors supplied by the user. The service reads labelled data in Weka format and the priors for each cue and class and computes $P(cue_i|k)$. The output of this web service can be directly used to classify new instances with the first one.

3 Test case: Lexical Acquisition

As a showcase, we will show our work in cue-based noun classification. The aim is the automatic acquisition of lexical semantic information by building classifiers for a number of lexical semantic classes.

3.1 Demonstration Outline

In our demonstration, we will show how we can use the web services to learn, tune and test Bayesian models for different lexical classes. We will compare our results with a Naive Bayes approach, which can also be learned with our system, using null virtual data.

First of all, we will get noun occurrences from a corpus and encode these occurrences as cue vectors applying a set of regular expressions. This will be done with another web service that directly outputs a Weka file. This Weka file will be divided into train and test data.

Secondly, the obtained training data will be used as input in the Bayesian learner web service, obtaining the values for $P(cue_i|k)$ for each cue and class. We will perform two calls: one using prior knowledge and one without it (MLE approach).

Finally, these two sets of parameters will be used to annotate the test data and we will compare the performance of the Bayesian model with the performance of the MLE model.

Acknowledgments

This work was funded by the EU 7FP project 248064 PANACEA.

References

J. Bybee. 1998. The emergent lexicon. CLS 34: The panels. *Chicago Linguistics Society*. 421-435.

N. Chater,and C.D. Manning. 2006. Probabilistic models of language processing and acquisition.*Trends in Cognitive Sciences*, 10, 335-344.

N. Chomsky.1980. Rules and representations. Oxford: Basil Blackwell.

A. E. Goldberg. 2006. Constructions at work. Oxford University Press.

T. L. Griffiths, C. Kemp, and J.B. Tenenbaum. 2008. Bayesian models of cognition. In Ron Sun (ed.), *Cambridge Handbook of Computational Cognitive Modeling*.Cambridge University Press.

D. J. C. MacKay. 2003. Information Theory, Inference, and Learning Algorithms. *Cambridge University Press,* 2003. ISBN 0-521-64298-1

R.J. Quinlan. 1993. C4.5: Programs for Machine Learning. *Series in Machine Learning*.Morgan Kaufman, San Mateo, CA.

Xu, F. and Tenenbaum, J. B. (2007).Word learning as Bayesian inference.*Psychological Review 114*(2).

G.K. Zipf. 1935. *The Psycho-Biology of Language*, Houghton Mifflin, Boston.

Unseen features.
Collecting semantic data from congenital blind subjects

Alessandro Lenci[♣], Marco Baroni[♠], Giovanna Marotta[♣]

[♣]University of Pisa (Italy)
[♠]University of Trento (Italy)
alessandro.lenci@ling.unipi.it, marco.baroni@unitn.it, gmarotta@ling.unipi.it

Congenital blind subjects are able to learn how to use color terms and other types of vision-related words in a way that is de facto undistinguishable from sighted people. It has actually been proposed that language provides a rich source of information that blind subjects can exploit to acquire aspects of word meaning that are related to visual experience, such as the color of fruits or animals. Despite this, whether and how sensory deprivation affects the structure of semantic representations is still an open question. In this talk, we present a new, freely available collection of feature norms produced by congenital blind subjects and normal sighted people. Subjects were asked to produce semantic features describing the meaning of concrete and abstract nouns and verbs. Data were collected from Italian subjects, translated into English, and categorized with respect to their semantic type (e.g. hypernym, meronym, physical property, etc.). First analyses of the feature norms highlight important differences between blind and sighted subjects, for instance for the role of color and other visual features in the produced semantic descriptions. This resource can provide new evidence on the role of perceptual experience in shaping concepts, as well as on its interplay with information extracted from linguistic data. The norms will also be used to carry out computational experiments with distributional semantic models to simulate blind and sighted semantic spaces.

PHACTS about activation-based word similarity effects

Basilio Calderone
CLLE-ERSS (UMR 5263) CNRS &
Université de Toulouse-Le Mirail
31058 Toulouse Cedex 9, France
basilio.calderone@univ-tlse2.fr

Chiara Celata
Scuola Normale Superiore
Laboratorio di Linguistica
56126 Pisa, Italy
c.celata@sns.it

Abstract

English phonotactic learning is modeled by means of the PHACTS algorithm, a topological neuronal receptive field implementing a phonotactic activation function aimed at capturing both local (i.e., phonemic) and global (i.e., word-level) similarities among strings. Limits and merits of the model are presented.

1 Introduction

Categorical rules and probabilistic constraints of phonotactic grammar affect speakers' intuitions about the acceptability of word-level units in a number of experimental tasks, including continuous speech segmentation and word similarity judgment. Several sources of information contribute to phonotactic generalization, including sub-segmental properties, segment transition probabilities, lexical neighborhood effects; all these factors have been independently or jointly modeled in several recent accounts of phonotactics and phonotactic learning (Coady and Aslin, 2004; Vitevitch, 2003; Vitevitch and Luce, 2005; Hayes and Wilson, 2008; Albright, 2009; Coetzee, 2009).

In this study, we explore the word level phonotactics in terms of a function of 'phonotactic activation' within a PHACTS environment (Celata et al., 2011). PHACTS is a topological neuronal receptive field implementing an n-gram sampling estimate of the frequency distribution of phonemes and a sub- lexical chunking of recurrent sequences of phonemes. Once this phonotactic knowledge has been developed, the model generalizes it to novel stimuli to derive activation-based representations of full lexical forms, thus mirroring the contribution of lexical neighborhood effects. Then the similarity values for pairs of words and non-words can be calculated.

2 PHACTS: the model

PHACTS (for PHonotactic ACTivation System) is based on the principles of a Self-Organizing Map (SOM) (Kohonen, 2000), an associative memory algorithm which realizes low-dimensional (generally, bi-dimensional) representations of a multidimensional input space.
PHACTS simulates the formation of phonotactic knowledge in the mind of a speaker, who is exposed to a stream of phonological words and gradually develops a mental representation of the statistical regularities shaping the phonotactics of a given language. The model also performs lexical generalizations on the basis of the phonotactic knowledge developed in the training phase.

The physical structure of PHACTS is defined by a set S (with finite cardinality) of neurons n_{jk} with $1 \leq j \leq J$ and $1 \leq k \leq K$ arranged in a bi-dimensional grid of $S = \{n_{11}, n_{12}, \dots n\}$, $\|S\| = JK$. Each neuron in the grid corresponds to a vector (the so-called prototype vector) whose dimension is equal to the dimension of the input data vector. At the beginning of the learning process, the prototype vectors assume random values while, as learning progresses, they change their values to fit the input data.

PHACTS works according to the two following phases: i) the training phase, where language-specific phonotactic knowledge is acquired; ii) the lexical generalization phase.

2.1 Training phase: the acquisition of phonotactic knowledge

At the beginning, each input word iteratively hits the system. For any iteration, the algorithm searches for the *best matching unit* (BMU), that is, the neuron which is topologically the closest to the input vector i and which is a good candidate to represent the input data through the prototype vector. The search for the BMU is given by maximizing the dot product of i and u_{jk} in the *t*-th step of the iteration:

$$BMU((i)t) = \arg\max_{jk}(\mathbf{i}(t) \cdot \mathbf{u}_{jk}) \quad (1)$$

In other terms, the $BMU((i)t)$ is the best aligned prototype vector with respect to the input i. After the BMU is selected for each i at time t, PHACTS adapts the prototype vector u_{jk} to the current input according to the topological adaptation equation given in (2):

$$\Delta u_{jk}(t) = \alpha(t)\delta(t)[i(t) - u_{jk}(t-1)] \quad (2)$$

where $\alpha(t)$ is a *learning rate* and $\delta(t)$ is the so-called *neighborhood function*. The *neighborhood function* is a function of time and distance between the BMU and each of its neighbors on the bi-dimensional map. It defines a set of neurons around the that would receive training, while neurons outside this set would not be changed. In our model the *neighborhood function* is defined as a Gaussian function.

The α parameter controls for the elasticity of the network, and δ roughly controls for the area around each best matching where the neurons are modified. The initial value of both parameters is set heuristically and in general decreases as long as the learning progresses. In order to facilitate a training convergence, we set $\alpha \rightarrow 0$ and $\delta \rightarrow 0$ as $t \rightarrow 0$. PHACTS performs a vector mapping of the data space in input to the output space defined by the prototype vectors u_{jk} on the bi-dimensional grid of neurons S.

2.1.1 The data: Type and token frequency in PHACTS

For the present simulations, PHACTS was trained on a portion of the CELEX English database (Baayen et al., 1995), and specifically on 8266 English word types phonologically transcribed and provided with their frequency of occurrence (only the words with token frequency > 100 were selected). Each phoneme was phonologically encoded according to a binary vector specifying place, manner of articulation and voicing for consonants, roundedness, height and anteriority for vowels. The bi-dimensional map was 25 X 35 neurons, and thus $S = 875$. Input words were sampled according to i for PHACTS is constituted by the input training words with a n-gram sampling window (with *n* spanning up the length of the longest word).

During the training phase, the map takes into account the global distribution of the n-grams in order to realize the topological activations of the phonotactic patterns ('phonotactic activation'). Both token frequency (i.e., the number of occurrences of specific n-grams) and type frequency (i.e., the number of all members of an n-gram type as defined by phonological features shared; for instance, */tan/* and */dim/* are two realizations of the trigram type *stop+vowel+nasal*) play a key role in phonotactic activation. By virtue of being repeatedly inputted to the map, a high token frequency n-gram will exhibit high activation state in the map. Low token frequency n-grams, however, will exhibit activation on the SOM only if they share phonological material (namely, phonemes or features) with high token frequency n-grams. Type frequency generates entrenchment effects in the map; high type frequency n-grams will occupy adjacent positions on the bi-dimensional map, thus defining clear phonotactic clusters. For these reasons, PHACTS differ sharply from current models of phonotactic learning, where only type frequencies are assumed to play a role in phonotactic generalization (and formalized accordingly). (Albright, 2009)

2.2 N-gram generalization and lexical generalizations

Once PHACTS has been exposed to an input of phonologically-encoded n-grams , an activation-based representation of unseen words can be derived. This phase implements a linear thresholded function d in which each neuron ŤfiresŢ as a function of its activation with respect to the (unseen) n-grams. In this sense each neuron acts as a 'transfer function'Ţ of an activation weight depending on the alignment between the unseen n-gram vector and the best aligned n-gram prototype vector.

Lexical generalization in PHACTS is therefore a word-level transfer process whereby the activation values of each word n-gram are summed according to equation [4]:

$$F_{\text{PHACTS}}(x) = \sum_{jk} \Phi(x) \quad (3)$$

The cumulative action of n-gram activations realizes a distributed representation of the word in which both phonological similarity (at the string level), and token frequency effects for phonotactic patterns are taken into account.
Being based on an associative memory learning of phonological words inputted by a n-gram sampling window, PHACTS develops topological cumulative memory traces of the learned words in which phonotactic activations emerge as the results of repeated mnemonic superimpositions of n-grams. This aspect is crucial for a distributional analysis of the morphotactic salience in a given language. In this direction, PHACTS was successfully implemented in the modeling of the micro- and macro-phonotactics in Italian (Calderone and Celata, 2010). By micro-phonotactics we mean sequential information among segments (e.g., the fact that, in the specific language, a phonological sequence, such as */ato/*, differs from similar sequences, such as */uto/*, */rto/*, and */atu/*). By macro-phonotactics we mean positional information within the word, i.e., sub-lexical (or chunk) effects (e.g., the fact that word-initial */#ato/* is different from word-medial */-ato-/*, as well as from word-final */ato#/*). In English language as well, PHACTS seems to distributionally distinguish a positional relevance for highly attested phonological sequences such as */ing/*. Figure 1 reports the phonotactic activation states outputted for the sequence */ing/* in initial and final word position (training corpus and parameters described in 2.1.1).

3 The experiments

According to the literature, the speakers in judging the wordlikeness of isolated non-words rely mainly on a grammar-based phonotactic knowledge and enhance the correspondence among types of strings (e.g., segmental features and onset and coda constituency). In doing so, they establish connections between each non-word and the

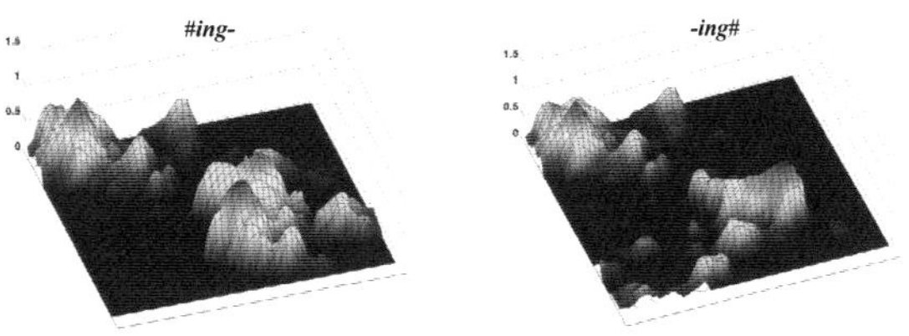

Figure 1: Phonotactic activation states for the sequence *#ing-* (initial word position) and *-ing#* (final word position)

neighborhood of all attested and unattested (but phonotactically legal, i.e., potentially attested) strings of their language. This must be a computationally hard task to accomplish even when no time restrictions are imposed, as in traditional wordlikeness experiments (since (Scholes, 1966) onward). In this experiment, we want to verify whether such task can be modeled in PHACTS and whether the vector representation of words outputted by PHACTS may represent a solid basis for this type of phonotactic evaluation. To evaluate PHACTS's ability to reproduce the typicality patterns produced by the speakers in judging the 'Englishness' of isolated strings, we had to derive a similarity value among each string and some counterpart in the English lexicon, as explained with more details below. We used 150 non-words, which were randomly selected from the list of 272 non-words of Bailey and Hahn (2001, B & H henceforth).

In that study, pronounceable non-words were created, either 4- or 5-phoneme long, differing from their nearest real word neighbor by either one or two phonemes (in terms of substitution, addition or subtraction). In the former case they were called near misses, in the latter case they were called isolates. 22 isolates and 250 near misses around the isolates were used in the B & H's study; 24 English speakers were asked to judge the 'Englishness' of the non-words that were individually presented in their orthographic and auditory form. The 150 non-words used in the present experiment were selected from among the near misses only. PHACTS was asked to derive the cosine value between the vector representations of each non- word and the corresponding real English words composing its neighbor family (according to the lists provided in B & H). The total number of string pairs was 1650 (the average number of neighbors for each non-word being 11). Then, an average cosine value was calculated for each of the 150 non-words. The average cosine value was assumed to reflect the phonotactic acceptability of each non-word with respect to their real word neighbors and therefore, to approximate the speakers' typicality judgment of isolated non-words. An edit distance calculation (normalized by the length of the two strings) was performed for the same 1650 pairs of non-words. Since the neighbors were all selected by adding, subtracting or modifying one phoneme from their reference non-words, the edit distance values were expected not to vary to a large extent. In the edit distance algorithm, values range from 0 to 1 according to the degree of the similarity between the two strings As expected, the distribution of the edit distance values was not uniform and the 1650 string pairs elicited a very small range of edit distance values. In total, 96% of cases elicited only four different edit distance values (namely, 0.83, 0.87, 0.93 and 0.97); the remaining 4% elicited three different values which were all higher than 0.7.

The cosine values outputted by PHACTS for the same string pairs were evaluated with respect to the calculated edit distances. As in the case of the edit distance algorithm, cosine values close to 1 indicate high similarity while values close to 0 indicate low similarity. As in the case of the edit distances, the cosine values were asymmetrically distributed, highly skewed to the right (for high similarity values). The global range of the distribution of values was similar for the two algorithms (spanning from 0.7 to 0.99). However, compared to the sharpness of the edit distance results (see Figure 2), PHACTS's output included subtler variations across comparisons, with fine distinctions distributed over a continuous range of values. The edit distance and the cosine values turned out to be correlated with $r = 0.465$. Although the nature of the difference between PHACTS's output and the edit distance algorithm should be better evaluated with respect to a more varied data set, also including pairs of very dissimilar strings, we could preliminarily conclude that the cosine value calculated by PHACTS for pairs of activation-based string representations did not correspond to an edit distance calculation.

We further verified whether PHACTS cosine values could approximate the perceived phonotac-

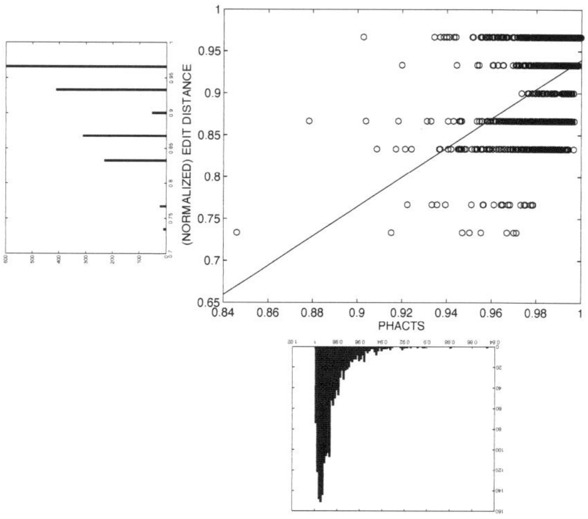

Figure 2: Correlation scatterplot and distribution histograms of the edit distance and PHACTS values for the B & H's materials

tic distance between two strings, as it is calculated by the speaker when (s)he is asked to judge the phonotactic acceptability of an isolated non-word. To test this hypothesis, the average cosine value of each non-word was correlated with the corresponding acceptability rating produced by the English subjects in the B & H's work. The Spearman's rank correlation between speakers' ratings and the (exp-transformed) cosine values was $\rho = .216, p < .01$. Although statistically significant, the correlation coefficient was rather low and revealed that the observed and simulated behaviors overlapped only to a limited extent. In particular, PHACTS did not reach a span of phonotactic acceptability as large as the speakers appeared to produce (with ratings comprised between 2.1 and 6.5).

In conclusion, PHACTS-based word similarity calculation appeared not to produce a reliable ranking of strings according to their phonotactic wellformedness. On the other hand, it did produce a fine-grained distributed representation of word in which both phonological similarity and token frequency effects for full forms seemed to define phonotactic activations of highly attested phonological sequences. This kind of representation differed from raw calculations of the number of operations required to transform a string into another.

Experimental protocols for modeling word similarity in PHACTS are currently under investigation.

References

Adam Albright. 2009. Feature-based generalisation as a source of gradient acceptability. *Phonology*, 26(1):9–41.

Harald R. Baayen, Richard Piepenbrock, and Leon Gulikers. 1995. The celex lexical database. release 2 (cd-rom). *Philadelphia: Linguistic Data Consortium, University of Philadelphia: Linguistic Data Consortium, University of Pennsylvania.*

Basilio Calderone and Chiara Celata. 2010. The morphological impact of micro- and macro-phonotactics. computational and behavioral analysis (talk given). In *14th International Morphology Meeting*, Budapest, 13-16 May.

Chiara Celata, Basilio Calderone, and Fabio Montermini. 2011. Enriched sublexical representations to access morphological structures. a psycho-computational account. *TAL-Traitement Automatique du Langage*, 2(52):123–149.

Jeffry A. Coady and Richard N. Aslin. 2004. Young children's sensitivity to probabilistic phonotactics in the developing lexicon. *Journal of Experimental Child Psychology*, 89:183–213.

Andries W. Coetzee. 2009. Grammar is both categorical and gradient. In S. Parker, editor, *Phonological Argumentation: Essays on Evidence and Motivation*. Equinox.

Bruce Hayes and Colin Wilson. 2008. A maximum entropy model of phonotactics and phonotactic learning. *Linguistic Inquiry*, 39(3):379–440.

Teuvo Kohonen. 2000. *Self-Organizing Maps*. Springer, Heidelberg.

Robert J. Scholes. 1966. *Phonotactic Grammaticality*. Mouton.

Michael S. Vitevitch and Paul A. Luce. 2005. Increases in phonotactic probability facilitate spoken nonword repetition. *Journal of Memory and Language*, 52(2):193–204.

Michael S. Vitevitch. 2003. The influence of sublexical and lexical representations on the processing of spoken words in english. *Clinical Linguistics & Phonetics*, 17:487–499.

I say have you say tem: profiling verbs in children data in English and Portuguese

Rodrigo Wilkens
Institute of Informatics
Federal University of Rio Grande do Sul
Brazil
rswilkens@inf.ufrgs.br

Aline Villavicencio
Institute of Informatics
Federal University of Rio Grande do Sul
Brazil
avillavicencio@inf.ufrgs.br

Abstract

In this paper we present a profile of verb usage across ages in child-produced sentences in English and Portuguese. We examine in particular lexical and syntactic characteristics of verbs and find common trends in these languages as children's ages increase, such as the prominence of general and polysemic verbs, as well as divergences such as the proportion of subject dropping. We also find a correlation between the age of acquisition and the number of complements of a verb for English.

1 Introduction

In this paper we report on a large scale investigation of some linguistic and distributional patterns of verbs in child-produced sentences for two languages, Portuguese and English. We compare the characteristics that emerge for two languages that, in spite of similarities in terms of verb usages also have important differences, in particular in allowing subject pro-drop, and examine to what degree these are reflected in the data. This is particularly relevant given the sparseness (and in some cases lack) of the Portuguese data, in particular for certain ages, which may not provide as clear indications as the English data, but existing analysis for the latter can also benefit the former and be used to help assess results obtained for similar trends found in it.

As such our work is related to that of Buttery and Korhonen (2007) who perform a large scale investigation of the subcategorization frames in the English corpora in CHILDES (MacWhinney, 2000), a database containing transcriptions of child-directed and child-produced sentences, comparing preferences in child and adult language to provide support for child language acquisition studies. These preferences are found using large amounts of automatically annotated data that would be otherwise too costly and time consuming to manually annotate.

At present, CHILDES contains data for more than 25 languages including English and Portuguese. For English, the corpora are currently available with annotations in raw, part-of-speech-tagged, lemmatized and parsed formats (Sagae et al., 2010) (Buttery and Korhonen, 2005) (Buttery and Korhonen, 2007). Although there are similar initiatives for other languages, like Spanish and Hebrew (Sagae et al., 2010), for Portuguese, there is a lack of such annotations on a large scale. In this work we address this issue and automatically annotate the Portuguese corpora with linguistic and distributional information using a robust statistical parser, providing the possibility of deeper analysis of language acquisition data.

Crosslinguistic investigations of child-produced language have also highlighted the important role of very general and frequent verbs, light verbs like *go, put* and *give* which are among the first to be acquired for languages like English and Italian as discussed by Goldberg (1999). In this paper we compare patterns found in child verb usage in English and Portuguese, in one of the first large scale investigations of syntactically annotated child-produced Portuguese data. Using this level of annotation we are able to examine patterns in verb usage in particular in terms of subjects and complements. Thus, this work is also related to the that of Valian (1991) who found a subject pro-drop rate of around 70% for 2 to 3 year old children in Italian, a pro-drop language, and even a significant number of subject omission for English, which is not a pro-drop language.

This investigation aims at producing a large-coverage profile of child verb usage that can inform computational models of language acquisition, by both reporting on preferences in child language as a whole and on a developmental level. This paper is structured as follows: in section 2 we report on the resources used for this investigation, and the results are discussed in section 3. We finish with some conclusions and future work.

2 Resources

For examining child-produced data we use the English and Portuguese corpora from CHILDES (MacWhinney, 2000). The English corpora in CHILDES have been parsed using at least three different pipelines: MOR, POST and MEGRASP (available as part of the CHILDES distribution, the corpora are POS tagged using the MOR and POST programs (Parisse and Normand, 2000)). In addition we use a version annotated with the RASP system (Briscoe et al., 2006), that tokenizes, tags, lemmatizes and parses the input sentences, outputting syntactic trees and then adding grammatical relations (GR) as described by (Buttery and Korhonen, 2005). This corpus contains 16,649 types and 76,386,369 tokens in 3,031,217 sentences distributed by age as shown in Table 1.

Table 1: Frequency of words and sentences by age in years in CHILDES for English and Portuguese

Age	English		Portuguese	
	Words (k)	Sent (k)	Words (k)	Sent (k)
0	4,944	130	0	0
1	12,124	604	7	2
2	19,481	1,367	8	1
3	17,962	468	0	0
4	16,725	249	1	61
5	3,266	121	38	1
6	782	19	47	1
7	1,088	63	56	1
8	12	5	56	1

The Portuguese, CHILDES contains 3 corpora: (1) Batoréo, with 60 narratives, 30 from adults and 30 from children, about two stories; (2) Porto Alegre with data from 5 to 9 year old children, collected both cross-sectionally and longitudinally; and (3) Florianópolis with the longitudinal data for one Brazilian child: 5530 utterances in broad phonetic transcription.

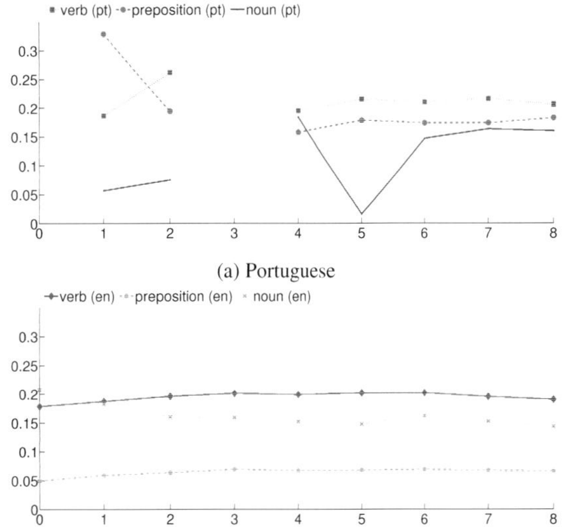

(a) Portuguese

(b) English

Figure 1: Verbs in relation to other frequent Parts-of-speech in English (1b) and Portuguese (1a)

The combined size of the Portuguese corpora in sentences and words is in Table 1. These were annotated with the PALAVRAS parser, a robust parser, which has a reported accuracy of 99% for part-of-speech tagging, 96-97% for syntactic trees, and 91.8% for multiword expressions (Bick, 2000)[1]. The childes annotation were first normalized to deal with incomplete words and remove transcription annotations, and then automatically lemmatized, POS tagged, parsed and assigned semantic tags for nouns, verbs and adjectives.

3 Verbs in children data

To characterize verb usage in each of these languages we examined the distribution of verbs across the ages in terms of their relative frequencies, the number of syntactic complements with which they occur, and looking at possible links between these and age of acquisition, as reported by Gilhooly and Logie (1980).

Figure 1 focuses on the relative distributions of verbs in relation to other frequent parts-of-speech: prepositions and nouns. For both languages verbs account for around 20% of the words used, and this proportion remains constant as age increases, with the exception of the discontinuity for years 3

[1]The PALAVRAS parser was evaluated using European and Brazilian Portuguese newspaper corpora (CETENFolha and CETEMPblico) composed of 9,368 sentences.

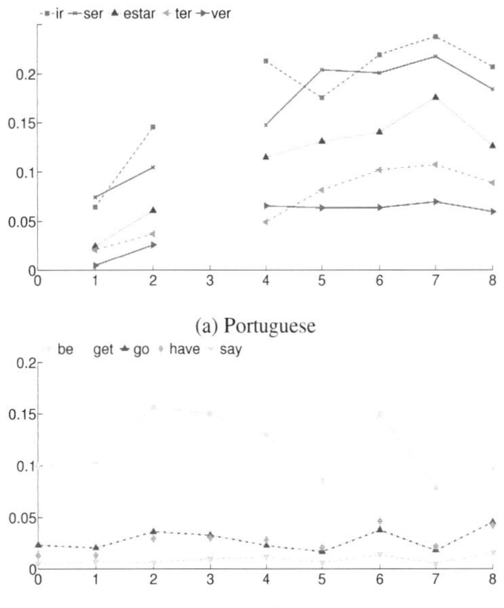

(a) Portuguese

(b) English

Figure 2: 5 most frequent verbs in Portuguese (2a) and in English (2b)

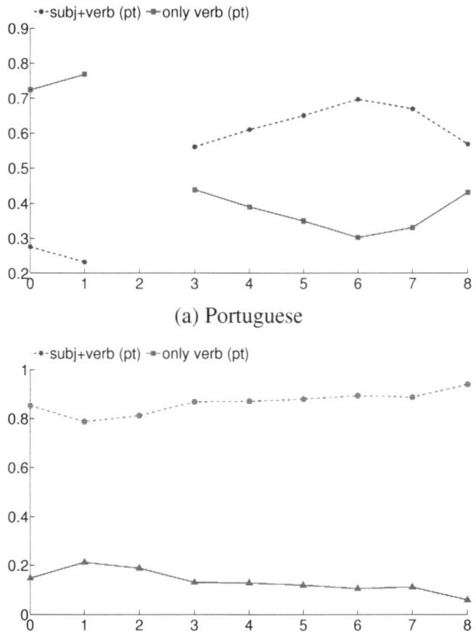

(a) Portuguese

(b) English

Figure 3: Percentage of sentences of verb with and without subject in Portuguese (3a) and in English (3b)

to 5 due to the lack of data for children with these ages in the Portuguese corpora in CHILDES.

Table 2: Verb types and tokens for English and Portuguese

Language	Types	Tokens
English	34,693	17,830,777
Portuguese	62,048	888,234

Table 2 shows the number of verb types and tokens in these two languages. Among these verbs, the top 5 most frequent verbs[2] for each language are: *be, get, go, have* and *say* for English and *ir* (go) *ser* (be) *estar* (be), *ter* (have) and *ver* (see) for Portuguese. These correspond to very general and polysemous verbs, and their relative proportions in the two languages remain high throughout the ages for children, figure 2. The frequencies for English are consistent with those reported by Goldberg (1999) and the Portuguese data is compatible with the crosslinguistic trends for related languages.

In terms of the syntactic characteristics of verbs in child-produced data, we examine separately the occurrence of subjects and other complements in these languages, using the syntactic annotation provided by the RASP and PALAVRAS parsers. In the RASP annotation (Briscoe, 2006) we search for 3 types of complements in English: a direct object (dobj), the second NP complement in a double object construction (obj2) and an indirect PP object (iobj). For Portuguese, we search the PALAVRAS annotation for the following types of objects: a direct (accusative) object (ACC), a dative object (DAT), an indirect prepositional object (PIV) and an object complement (OC).[3]

For subjects figure 3 shows the occurrences of overt (subj verb) and omitted subjects (only verb) in sentences in relation to the total number of verbs (verb) for the two languages. These are a source of divergence between them as in the English data most of the verb usages consistently have an overt subject, and only around 10-20% omit the subject, but these tend to occur less as the age increases, with a peak for 2 year old children. In Portuguese, on the other hand, initially most of the verb usages omit the subject, and only later

[2]The reported frequency for each verb is for the lemmatized form, including all its inflected forms.

[3]http://beta.visl.sdu.dk/visl/pt/info/symbolset-manual.html

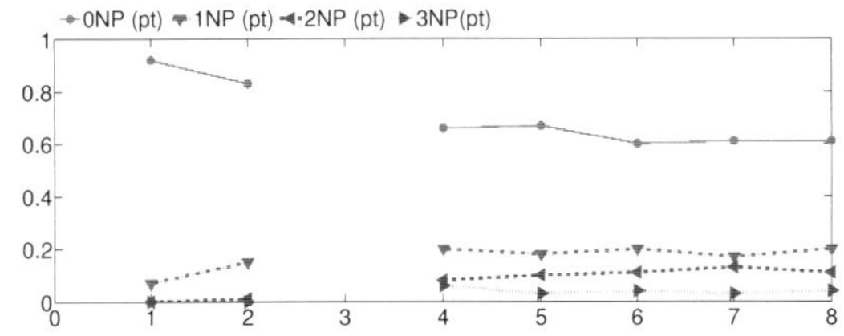

(a) Portuguese

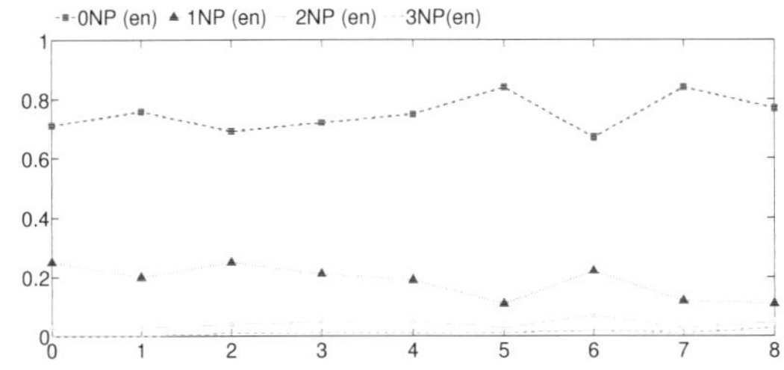

(b) English

Figure 4: Percentage of occurrence of objects in Portuguese (4a) and in English (4b)

this trend is reversed, but still maintaining a high proportion of subject dropping, around 40% of verb usages, and around 60% including an overt subject. The precise age for this change cannot be assessed from this data, due to the lack of sentences for 3-5 year old children in the Portuguese data. This difference between the two languages can be explained as a result of Portuguese being a (subject) pro-drop language and children being consistently exposed to subject dropping in their linguistic environment. Although English is not a pro-drop language, children, especially at an early age, still produce sentences without overt subjects, as much discussed in the literature (Valian, 1991) and more recently (Yang, 2010). Children learning pro-drop languages seem to adopt it from an early age and use it with a frequency much closer to adult usage (Valian, 1991).

In relation to other verb complements, we examine the changes in the distribution of verbs and their subcategorization frames in the corpus across children's ages. Figure 4 shows the distribution per age for verbs with one, two and three complements for both languages. As expected in general verbs with fewer complements are more frequently used and as the number of complements increases, the frequency decreases, for all ages and for both languages. Moreover, as age increases, there is a slight but constant increase in the presence of verbs with 2 and 3 complements in the corpus, with a small decrease in those with only 1, which nonetheless still account for the majority of the cases. These patterns are more clearly visible for English, as more data is available than for Portuguese for all ages.

To further investigate this we analyzed whether a relation between the number of complements of a verb and its age of acquisition could be found. For English we used the age of acquisition (AoA) scores from Gilhooly and Logie (1980) which is available for 22 of the verbs in the English data, but from these two verbs were removed from the set, as they did not occur in all the ages. For Portuguese, the scores from Marques et al. (2007) are available for only four verbs in the CHILDES corpora, and were therefore not considered in this analysis. Using the total frequency for a verb in the corpus, we calculated the relative frequencies for each number of complements (0, 1, 2 and 3) per age. For each verb and each age the number of complements with maximum frequency was used as the basis for checking if a correlation with the AoA scores for the verb could be found. In terms of the number of complements per age these verbs can be divided into 3 groups, apart from 2 of the verbs (*lock and burn*) that do not have any clear pattern:

0-obj: for verbs that are used predominantly without complements throughout the ages, *think, speak, swim, lie, turn, fly, try*;

1-obj: for verbs that appear consistently with 1 complement for all ages, *drive, chop, hate, find, win, tear*;

0-to-1: for verbs initially used mostly without complements but then consistently with 1 complement, *hurt, guess, throw, kick, hide*.

In terms of the age of acquisition, verbs in the 0-obj group tend to have lower scores than those in the second group, with a 0.72 Spearman's rank correlation coefficient indicating a high correlation between AoA and predominant number of complements of a verb. As the third group had both patterns, it was not considered in the analysis. These results suggest that the number of syntactic objects tends to increase with the age of acquisition. This may be partly explained by a potential increase in complexity as the number of obligatory arguments for a verb increase (Boynton-Hauerwas, 1998). However, more investigation is needed to confirm this trend.

4 Conclusions

In this paper we presented a wide-coverage profile of verbs in child-produced data, for English and Portuguese. We examined the distribution of some lexical and syntactic characteristics of verbs in these languages. Common trends, such as the prominent role of very general and polysemic verbs among the most frequently used and a preference for smaller number of complements were found throughout the ages in both languages. Divergences between them such as the proportion of subject dropping in each language were also found: a lower proportion for English which decreases with age and a higher proportion for Portuguese which remains relatively high. These results are compatible with those reported by e.g. Goldberg (1999) and Valian (1991), respectively. Furthermore, for English we found a high correlation between a lower age of acquisition of a verb and a lower predominant number of complements. Given the size of the Portuguese data, for some of these analyses further investigation is needed with more data to confirm the trends found.

For future work we intend to extend these analyses for other parts-of-speech, particularly nouns, also looking at other semantic and pragmatic factors, such as polysemy, concreteness and familiarity. In addition, we plan to examine intrinsic (e.g. length of words; imageability; and familiarity) and and extrinsic factors (e.g. frequency), and their effect in groups with typical development and with specific linguistic impairments.

References

Bick, E. 2000. *The Parsing System Palavras. Automatic Grammatical Analysis of Portuguese in a Constraint Grammar Framework.* [S.l.]: University of Arhus.

Bick, E. 2003. *Multi-level NER for Portuguese in a CG framework.* Proceedings of the Computational Processing of the Portuguese Language.

Boynton-Hauerwas, L. S. 1998. *The role of general all purpose verbs in language acquisition: A comparison of children with specific language impairments and their language-matched peers.* Northwestern University

Briscoe, E., Carroll, J., and Watson, R. 2006. *The second release of the rasp system.* COLING/ACL 2006 Interactive Presentation Sessions, Sydney, Australia.

Briscoe, T. 2006. *An introduction to tag sequence grammars and the RASP system parser.* Technical report in University of Cambridge, Computer Laboratory.

Buttery, P., Korhonen, A. 2005. *Large Scale Analysis of Verb Subcategorization differences between Child Directed Speech and Adult Speech.* Interdisciplinary Workshop on the Identification and Representation of Verb Features and Verb Classes.

Buttery, P., Korhonen, A. 2007. *I will shoot your shopping down and you can shoot all my tins– Automatic Lexical Acquisition from the CHILDES Database.* Proceedings of the Workshop on Cognitive Aspects of Computational Language Acquisition. Association for Computational Linguistics.

Gilhooly, K.J. and Logie, R.H. 1980. *Age of acquisition, imagery, concreteness, familiarity and ambiguity measures for 1944 words.* Behaviour Research Methods and Instrumentation.

Goldberg, Adele E. . *The Emergence of Language*, chapter Emergence of the semantics of argument structure constructions, pages 197–212. Carnegie Mellon Symposia on Cognition Series.

Hsu, A. S., Chater, N. 2010. *Aspects of the Theory of Syntax.* MIT Press.

MacWhinney, B. 2000. *The CHILDES project: tools for analyzing talk.* Lawrence Erlbaum Associates, second edition.

Marques, J. F., Fonseca, F. L., Morais, A. S., Pinto, I. A. 2007. *Estimated age of acquisition norms for 834 Portuguese nouns and their relation with other psycholinguistic variables.* Behavior Research Methods.

Parisse, C. and Normand, M. T. Le. 2000. *Automatic disambiguation of the morphosyntax in spoken language corpora.* Behavior Research Methods, Instruments, and Computers.

Pavio, A., Yuille, J.C., and Madigan, S.A. 1968. *Concreteness, imagery and meaningfulness values for 925 words.* Journal of Experimental Psychology Monograph Supplement.

Sagae, K., Davis, E., Lavie, A., MacWhinney, B. and Wintner, S. 2010. *Morphosyntactic annotation of CHILDES transcripts.* Journal of Child Language.

Toglia, M.P. and Battig, W.R. 1978. *Handbook of Semantic Word Norms.* New York: Erlbaum.

Valian, V. 1991. *Syntactic subjects in the early speech of American and Italian Children.* Journal of Cognition.

Yang, Charles 2010. *Three factors in language variation.* Lingua.

Get out but don't fall down: verb-particle constructions in child language

Aline Villavicencio[♣♠], Marco A. P. Idiart[♣], Carlos Ramisch[♣], Vítor Araújo[♣], , Beracah Yankama[♠], Robert Berwick[♠]

[♣]Federal University of Rio Grande do Sul (Brazil)
[♠]MIT (USA)

alinev@gmail.com, marco.idiart@gmail.com, ceramisch@inf.ufrgs.br, vbuaraujo@inf.ufrgs.br, beracah@mit.edu, berwick@csail.mit.edu

Abstract

Much has been discussed about the challenges posed by Multiword Expressions (MWEs) given their idiosyncratic, flexible and heterogeneous nature. Nonetheless, children successfully learn to use them and eventually acquire a number of Multiword Expressions comparable to that of simplex words. In this paper we report a wide-coverage investigation of a particular type of MWE: verb-particle constructions (VPCs) in English and their usage in child-produced and child-directed sentences. Given their potentially higher complexity in relation to simplex verbs, we examine whether they appear less prominently in child-produced than in child-directed speech, and whether the VPCs that children produce are more conservative than adults, displaying proportionally reduced lexical repertoire of VPCs or of verbs in these combinations. The results obtained indicate that regardless of any additional complexity VPCs feature widely in children data following closely adult usage. Studies like these can inform the development of computational models for language acquisition.

1 Introduction

There has been considerable discussion about the challenges imposed by Multiword Expressions (MWEs) which in addition to crossing word boundaries act as a single lexical unit at some levels of linguistic analysis (Calzolari et al., 2002; Sag et al., 2002; Fillmore, 2003). They include a wide range of grammatical constructions such as verb-particle constructions (VPCs), idioms, compound nouns and listable word configurations, such as terminology and formulaic linguistic units (Wray, 2009). Depending on the definition, they may also include less traditional sequences like *copy of* in *They gave me a copy of the book* (Fillmore et al., 1988), greeting formulae like *how do you do?*, and lexical bundles such as *I dont know whether* or memorized poems and familiar phrases from TV commercials (Jackendoff, 1997). These expressions may have reduced syntactic flexibility, and be semantically more opaque so that their semantics may not be easily inferred from their component words. For instance, to *play down X* means to *(try to) make X seem less important than it really is* and not literally a playing event.

These expressions may also breach general syntactic rules, sometimes spanning phrasal boundaries and often having a high degree of lexicalisation and conventionality. They form a *complex of features that interact in various, often untidy, ways and represent a broad continuum between non-compositional (or idiomatic) and compositional groups of words* (Moon, 1998). In addition, they are usually sequences or groups of words that co-occur more often than would be expected by chance, and have been argued to appear in the same order of magnitude in a speaker's lexicon as the simplex words (Jackendoff, 1997).

In terms of language acquisition difficulties may arise as the interpretation of these expressions often demands more knowledge than just about (1) unitary words and (2) word-to-word relations. This introduces a distinction between what a learner is able to computationally disambiguate or figure out automatically from language and what must be explicitly stored/memorized and *retrieved whole from memory at the time of use, rather than being subject to generation or analysis by the language grammar* (Wray, 2009, p. 9). Yet, according to Fillmore et al. (1988), in an ideal learning environment, most of the knowledge about how to use a language should be computable while explicitly memorized sequences should be kept to a minimum.

Due to these idiosyncrasies they have been noted as easily phonetically mislearned: e.g. *by and large* mistaken for *by in large, to all intents and purposes* for *to all intensive purposes*, and *an arm and a leg* for *a nominal egg* (Fillmore, 2003). For second language (L2) learners in particular (Wray, 2002) MWEs are indeed a well-known cause of problems and less likely to be used by them than by native speakers in informal spoken contexts (Siyanova and Schmitt, 2007). Even if L2 learners may be capable of producing a large number of MWEs, their underlying intuitions and fluency do not match those of native speakers (Siyanova and Schmitt, 2008) and they may produce marked combinations that are not conventionally used together (e.g. plastic surgery/?operation, strong/?powerful tea) (Pearce, 2002; Siyanova and Schmitt, 2007).

Given the potential additional sources of complexity of MWEs for learning, in this paper we investigate whether children shy away from using them when they communicate. We focus on a particular type of MWEs, VPCs, which present a wide range of syntactic and semantic idyosincrasies examining whether children produce proportionally less VPCs than adults. In addition, we analyze whether any potential added processing costs for VPCs are reflected in a reduced choice of VPCs or verbs to form these combinations in child-produced sentences compared to adult usage. Finally, given the possibility of flexible word orders in VPCs with the verb and particle not only occurring adjacently but also with an NP object between them, we compare these two groups in terms of distances between the verb and the particle in these combinations, to determine whether there is a preference for a joint or a split configuration and if children and adults adopt distinct strategies for their usage. By profiling the VPC usage by children our aim is to provide the basis for a computational modeling of the acquisition of these constructions.

This paper is structured as follows: in section 2 describes VPCs and related works; section 3 presents the resources and methods used in this paper. The analyses of VPCs in children and adults sentences are in section 4. We finish with conclusions and possibilities of future works.

2 Related Work

VPCs are combinations of verbs and prepositional (*up, down, ...*), adverbial (*away, back,...*), adjectival (*short,...*) or verbal (*go, be,...*) particles, and in this work we focus on VPCs with prepositional or adverbial particles like *put off* and *move on*. From a language acquisition perspective, the complexity of VPCs arises from their wide syntactic as semantic variability.

Syntactically, like simplex verbs, VPCs can occur in different subcategorisation frames (e.g. intransitive in *break down* and transitive in *print NP up*). However, the type of verb and the number of arguments of a VPC seem to have an impact in learning as both children with typical development and with specific language impairments (SLI) seem to use obligatory arguments and inflectional morphology more consistently with general all purpose verbs, like *make, go, do, put*, than with more specific verbs. Moreover, as the number of obligatory arguments increases children with SLI seem to produce more general and fewer specific verbs (Boynton-Hauerwas, 1998). Goldberg (1999b) refers to these verbs as light verbs, suggesting that due to their frequency of use, they are acquired earlier by children, and subsequently act as centers of gravity from which more specific instances can be learnt. These verbs are very common and frequent in the everyday communication, that could be used in place of more specialized instances (e.g. *make* instead of *build*).

In transitive VPCs there is the additional difficulty of the particle appearing in different word orders in relation to the verb: in a joint configuration, adjacent to the verb (e.g. *make up NP*) or in a split configuration after the NP complement (*make NP up*) (Lohse et al., 2004). While some VPCs can appear in both configurations, others are inseparable (*run across NP*), and a learner has to successfully account for these. Gries (2002) using a multifactorial analysis to investigate 25 variables that could be linked to particle placement like size of the direct object (in syllables and words), type of NP (pronoun or lexical), type of determiner (indefinite or definite). For a set of 403 VPCs from the British National Corpus he obtains 84% success in predicting (adult) native speakers' choice. Lohse et al. (2004) propose that these factors can be explained by considerations of processing efficiency based on the size of the object NP and on semantic dependencies among the verb, the particle, and the object. In a similar study for children Diessel and Tomasello (2005) found that the type of the NP (pronoun vs lexical NP) and semantics of the particle (spatial vs non-spatial) were good predictors of placement on child language data.

Semantically, one source of difficulties for learners comes from the wide spectrum of compositionality that VPCs present. On one end of the spectrum some combinations like *take away* compositionally combine the meaning of a verb with the core meaning of a particle giving a sense of motion-through-location (Bolinger, 1971). Other VPCs like *boil up* are semi-idiomatic (or aspectual) and the particle modifies the meaning of the verb adding a sense of completion or result. At the other end of the spectrum, idiomatic VPCs like *take off*, meaning *to imitate* have an opaque meaning that cannot be straightforwardly inferred from the meanings of each of the components literally. Moreover, even if some verbs form combinations with almost every particle (e.g., *get, fall, go,...*), others are selectively combined with only a few particles (e.g., *book* and *sober* with *up*), or do not combine well with them at all (e.g., *know, want, resemble,...*) (Fraser, 1976). Although there are some semi-productive patterns in these combinations, like verbs of cooking and the aspectual *up* (*cook up, boil up, bake up*), and stative verbs not forming VPCs, for a learner it may not be clear whether an unseen combination of verb and particle is indeed a valid VPC that can be produced or not. Sawyer (1999) longitudinal analysis of VPCs in child language found that children seem to treat aspectual and compositional combinations differently, with the former being more frequent and employing a larger variety of types than the latter. The sources of errors also differ and while for compositional cases the errors tend to be lexical, for aspectuals there is a predominance of syntactic errors such as object dropping, which accounts for 92% of the errors in split configuration for children under 5 (Sawyer, 1999). Children with SLI tended to produce even more object dropping errors for VPCs than children with typical development, despite both groups producing equivalent numbers of VPCs (Juhasz and Grela, 2008). Given that compositionality seems to have an impact on learning, to help reduce avoidance of phrasal verbs Sawyer (2000) proposes a semantic driven approach for second language learning where transparent compositional cases would be presented first to help familiarization with word order variation, semi-idiomatic cases would be taught next in groups according to the contribution of the particle (e.g telicity or completiveness), and lastly the idiomatic cases that need to be memorized.

In this paper we present a wide coverage examination of VPC distributions in child produced and child-directed sentences, comparing whether children reproduce the linguistic environment to which they are exposed or whether they present distinct preferences in VPC usage.

3 Materials and Methods

For this work we use the English corpora from the CHILDES database (MacWhinney, 1995) containing transcriptions of child-produced and child-directed speech from interactions involving children of different age groups and in a variety of settings, from naturalistic longitudinal studies to task oriented latitudinal cases. These corpora are available in raw, part-of-speech-tagged, lemmatized and parsed formats (Sagae et al., 2010). Moreover the English CHILDES Verb Construction Database (ECVCD) (Villavicencio et al., 2012) also adds for each sentence the RASP parsing and grammatical relations (Briscoe and Carroll, 2006), verb semantic classes (Levin, 1993), age of acquisition, familiarity, frequency (Coltheart, 1981) and other psycholinguistic and distributional characteristics. These annotated sentences are divided into two groups according to the speaker annotation available in CHILDES, the **Adults Set** and the **Children Set** contain respectively all the sentences spoken by adults and by children[1], as shown in table 1 as Parsed.

VPCs in these corpora are detected by looking in the RASP annotation for all occurrences of verbs followed by particles, prepositions and adverbs up to 5 words to the right, following Baldwin (2005), shown as Sentences with VPCs

[1]For the latter sentences which did not contain information about age were removed.

Sentences	Children Set	Adults Set
Parsed	482,137	988,101
with VPCs	44,305	83,098
with VPCs Cleaned	38,326	82,796
% with VPCs	7.95	8.38

Table 1: VPCs in English Corpora in the Children and Adults Sets

in table 1. The resulting sentences are subsequently automatically processed to remove noise and words mistagged as verbs. For these candidates with non-alphabetic characters, like @ in *a@l up*, were removed as were those that did not involve verbs (e.g. *di, dat,*), using the Comlex Lexicon as reference for verb validity (Macleod and Grishman, 1998). The resulting sets are listed as Sentences with VPCs Cleaned in table 1. The analyses reported in this paper use these sentences, and the distribution of VPCs per children age group is shown in table 2. Given the non-uniform amounts of VPC for each age group, and the larger proportion of VPC sentences in younger ages in these corpora, we consider children as a unique group. For these, the individual frequencies of the verb, the particle and the VPC are collected separately in the children set and in the adult set, using the mwetoolkit (Ramisch et al., 2010).

Age in months	VPC Sentences
0-24	2,799
24-48	26,152
48-72	8,038
72-96	1,337
>96	514
No age	4,841

Table 2: VPCs in Children Set per Age

To evaluate the VPCs in these sets, we use:

- English VPC dataset (Baldwin, 2008); which lists 3,078 VPCs with valency (intransitive and transitive) information;
- Comlex lexicon (Macleod and Grishman, 1998) containing 10,478 phrasal verbs;
- the Alvey Natural Language Tools (ANLT) lexicon (Carroll and Grover, 1989) with 6,351 phrasal verbs.

4 VPCs in Child Language

To investigate whether any extra complexity in the acquisition of VPCs is reflected in their reduced presence in child-produced than in child-directed sentences, we compare the proportion of VPCs in the Children and Adults Sets, table 3. In absolute terms adults produced more than double the number of VPCs that children did. However, given the differences in size of the two sets, in relative terms there was a similar proportion of VPC usage in these corpora for each of the groups: 7.95% of the sentences produced by children contained VPCs vs 8.38% of those by adults. Moreover, the frequencies with which these VPCs are used by both children and adults reflects the Zipfian distribution found for the use of words in natural languages, with a large part of the VPCs occurring just once in the data, table 4. In addition, in terms of frequency, children's production of VPCs resembles that of the adults.

Total VPC	Children Set	Adults Set
Tokens	38,326	82,796
Types	1,579	2,468

Table 3: VPC usage in CHILDES

Frequency	Children Set	Adults Set
1	42.62%	43.03%
2	13.05%	15%
3	8.36%	6.48%
4	4.05%	4.5%
≥5	31.92%	31%

Table 4: VPC types per frequency

Another possible source of divergence between children and adults is in the lexical variety found in VPCs. The potential difficulties with VPCs may be manifested in children producing a reduced repertoire of VPCs or using a smaller set of verbs to form these combinations. As shown in table 3, adults, as expected, employ a larger VPC vocabulary with 1.56 more types than children. However, an examination of the distributions of types reveals that they only differ by a scale. As a result when children frequencies are multiplied by a factor of 2.16, which corresponds to the ratio between VPC tokens used by adults and children (table 3), the resulting distribution has a very good match with the adult distribution, see figure 1. Therefore, the lower number of VPC types used by children can be explained totally by the lower number of sentences they produced, and the hypothesis that difficulties in VPCs would lead to their avoidance is not confirmed by the data.

Nonetheless, there is a discrepancy between the distributions found for the higher frequency VPCs. Children have a more uniform distribution and adults tend to repeat more often the higher frequency combinations (top left corner of figure 1). An evidence that this discrepancy is particular for high frequency VPCs, and not their constituent verbs, is shown in figure 2. This figure displays the rank plot for the verbs present in the VPCs, for both adults and children. The same scale factor used in figure 1 is applied to compensate for the lower number of VPC sentences in the children set. This time the match is extraordinary, spanning the whole vocabulary.

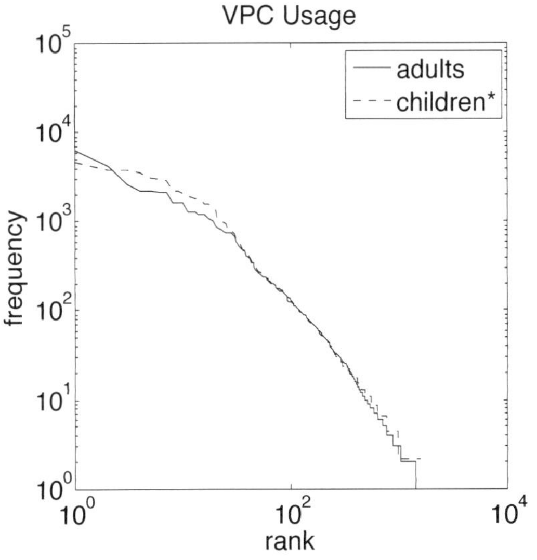

Figure 1: VPC Usage Frequency vs Ranking. The children frequency is scaled to match adult total VPC usage.

Ranks however, might not tell the whole story. It is important to verify if the same VPCs and verbs are present in the both vocabularies, and further if their orders in the ranks are similar. The two groups have very similar preferences for VPC usage, with a Kendall τ score of 0.63 which indicates that they are highly correlated, as Kendall τ ranges from -1 to 1. Furthermore they use a very similar set of verbs in VPCs, with a Kendall

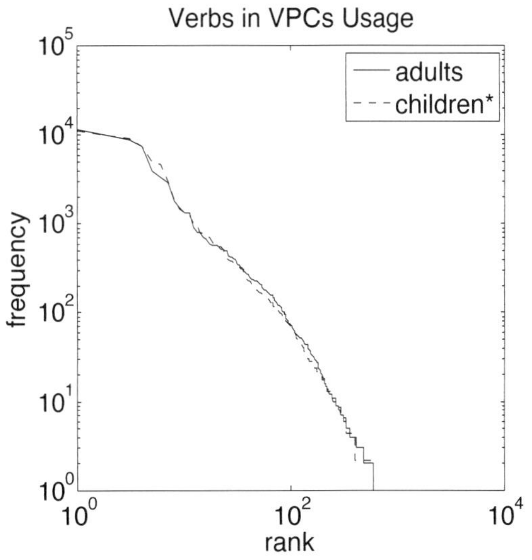

Figure 2: Verbs in VPCs Usage Frequency vs Ranking. The children frequency is scaled to match adult total VPC usage.

τ score of 0.84 pointing to a very strong correlation. We find less agreement between the orders of VPCs and verbs for both children and adults, indicating that the order of the verbs in the data is not predictive of the relative frequencies of VPCs. We examined (a) if children's VPC ranks followed their verb ranks, (b) if adults VPC ranks followed their verb ranks and (c) if children's VPC ranks followed adults' verb ranks. The resulting Kendall scores were around 0.2 for all three cases. Moreover, if the lower frequency VPCs are removed to avoid potential cases of noise, the Kendall τ score for VPCs by adults and children increases with the threshold, second line from the top in Figure 3, while it remains constant for all the other cases. As an example, the top 10 VPC types used by children and adults are listed in table 5. From these, 9 out of the 10 are the same differing only in the order in which they appear. Most of these combinations are listed in one of the dictionaries used for evaluation: 72% for adults and 75.87% for children. When a threshold of at least 5 counts is applied these values go up to 87.72% for adults and 79.82% for children, as would be expected. This indicates that besides any possible lack of coverage for child-directed VPCs in the lexicons or noise, it is in the lower frequency combinations that novel and domains specific non-standard usages can be found. Some

Rank	Chidren VPC	Children Freq	Adult VPC	Adult Freq	Child Rank
1	put on	2005	come on	6244	7
2	go in	1608	put on	4217	1
3	get out	1542	go on	2660	9
4	take off	1525	get out	2251	3
5	fall down	1329	take off	2249	4
6	put in	1284	put in	2177	6
7	come on	1001	sit down	2133	8
8	sit down	981	go in	1661	2
9	go on	933	come out	1654	10
10	come out	872	pick up	1650	18

Table 5: Top VPCs for Children and Adults

of the combinations not found in these dictionaries include *crawl in* and *creep up* by adults and *erase off* and *crash down* by children.

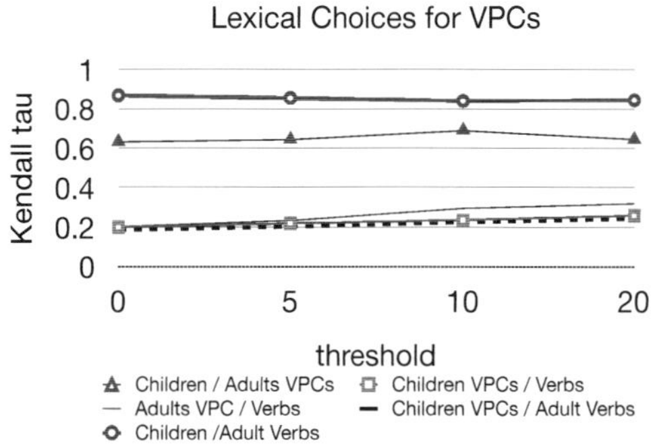

Figure 3: Kendall τ score per VPC frequency threshold

Finally, despite adults having a larger verb vocabulary used in VPCs than children, the two groups have similar ratios of verb per VPCs: 2.81 VPCs for children and 2.79 for adults, table 6. The top verbs used in VPCs types are also responsible for very frequent VPC tokens (e.g. *go, get, come, take, put, make and move*) accounting for 5.83% VPC types and 43.76% tokens for adults and 7.02% of the types and 47.81% of the tokens for children, confirming the discrepancy discussed earlier. These are very general verbs and some of the most frequent in the data, reported among the first to be learned (Goldberg, 1999a) which may facilitate their acquisition and use in VPCs.

Comparing VPC types used by children and by adults, this trend is confirmed: a large proportion (72.32%) of the VPC types that children use is also used by adults, Children ∩ Adult in table 6. When low frequency VPCs types are removed, this proportion increases (89.48%). Moreover, when the VPCs used only by the adults are considered, most of these (93.44%) occur with frequency lower than 5. This suggests that children tend to follow quite closely the combinations employed by adults, and the lower frequency cases may not yet be incorporated in their active vocabulary.

In terms of the distance between verb and particle, there is a strong preference in the data for joint combinations for both children and adults, table 7. For the split cases, the majority contains only one word between the verb and the particle. Children in particular display a slight dispreference for longer distances between verbs and particles, and over 97% of VPCs have at most 2 words between them.

Distance	Children Set	Adults Set
0	65.13%	64.14%
1	23.48%	22.15%
2	9.33%	10.90%
3	1.65%	2.15%
4	0.29%	0.47%
5	0.09%	0.16%

Table 7: Distance between verb and particle

5 Conclusions and future work

In this paper we presented an investigation of VPCs in child-produced and child-directed sentences in English to determine whether potential complexities in the nature of these combinations

	Children VPCs	Adult VPCs	Children ∩Adult VPCs	Children only VPCs	Adult only VPCs
VPCs	1579	2468	1142	437	1243
Verb in VPCs	561	884	401	160	483
Particle in VPCs	28	35	24	4	9
VPCs ≥ 5	504	766	451	53	278
Verb in VPCs ≥ 5	207	282	183	24	99
Particle in VPCs ≥ 5	18	20	17	1	3

Table 6: Number of VPC, Verb and Particle types by group, common usages

are reflected in their reduced usage by children. The combination of these results shows that, despite any additional difficulties, VPCs are as much a feature in children's data as in adults'. Children follow very closely adult usage in terms of the types and are sensitive to their frequencies, displaying similar distributions to adults. They also seem to use them in a similar manner in terms of particle placement. Therefore no correction for VPC complexity was found in this data.

Despite these striking similarities in many of the distributions, there are still some discrepancies between these two groups. In particular in the VPC ranks, children present a more uniform distribution for higher frequency VPCs when compared to adults. Moreover, there is a modest but significant dispreference for longer distances between verb and particle for children. Whether these reflect different strategies or efficiency considerations deserves to be further investigated.

Acknowledgements

This research was partly supported by CNPq Projects 551964/2011-1, 202007/2010-3, 305256/2008-4 and 309569/2009-5.

References

Timothy Baldwin. 2005. Deep lexical acquisition of verb-particle constructions. *Computer Speech & Language Special issue on MWEs*, 19(4):398–414.

Timothy Baldwin. 2008. A resource for evaluating the deep lexical acquisition of english verb-particle constructions. In *Proceedings of the LREC Workshop Towards a Shared Task for Multiword Expressions (MWE 2008)*, pages 1–2, Marrakech, Morocco, June.

Dwight Bolinger. 1971. *The phrasal verb in English*. Harvard University Press, Harvard, USA.

L. S. Boynton-Hauerwas. 1998. The role of general all purpose verbs in language acquisition: A comparison of children with specific language impairments and their language-matched peers. 59.

Ted Briscoe and John Carroll. 2006. Evaluating the accuracy of an unlexicalized statistical parser on the PARC depbank. In *Proceedings of the 21st International Conference on Computational Linguistics and 44th Annual Meeting of the Association for Computational Linguistics (COLING/ACL 2006)*, pages 41–48, Sidney, Australia, July. Association for Computational Linguistics.

Nicoleta Calzolari, Charles Fillmore, Ralph Grishman, Nancy Ide, Alessandro Lenci, Catherine Macleod, and Antonio Zampolli. 2002. Towards best practice for multiword expressions in computational lexicons. In *Third International Conference on Language Resources and Evaluation (LREC 2002)*, pages 1934–1940, Las Palmas, Canary Islands, Spain. European Language Resources Association.

John Carroll and Claire Grover. 1989. The derivation of a large computational lexicon of English from LDOCE. In B. Boguraev and E. Briscoe, editors, *Computational Lexicography for Natural Language Processing*. Longman.

M. Coltheart. 1981. The MRC psycholinguistic database. *Quarterly Journal of Experimental Psychology*, 33A:497–505.

Holger Diessel and Michael Tomasello. 2005. Particle placement in early child language : A multifactorial analysis. *Corpus Linguistics and Linguistic Theory*, 1(1):89–112.

Charles J. Fillmore, Paul Kay, and Mary C. O'Connor. 1988. Regularity and idiomaticity in grammatical constructions: The case of Let Alone. *Language*, 64(3):510–538.

Charles Fillmore. 2003. Multiword expressions: An extremist approach. Presented at Collocations and idioms 2003: linguistic, computational, and psycholinguistic perspectives.

Bruce Fraser. 1976. *The Verb-Particle Combination in English*. Academic Press, New York, USA.

Adele E. Goldberg, 1999a. *The Emergence of Language*, chapter Emergence of the semantics of argument structure constructions, pages 197–212. Carnegie Mellon Symposia on Cognition Series.

Adele E. Goldberg. 1999b. The emergence of the semantics of argument structure constructions. In B. MacWhinney, editor, *Emergence of language*. Lawrence Erlbaum Associates, Hillsdale, NJ.

Stefan Gries. 2002. The influence of processing on syntactic variation: Particle placement in english. In Nicole Dehé, Ray Jackendoff, Andrew McIntyre, and Silke Urban, editors, *Verb-Particle Explorations*, pages 269–288. New York: Mouton de Gruyter.

Ray Jackendoff. 1997. Twistin' the night away. *Language*, 73:534–559.

C. R. Juhasz and B. Grela. 2008. Verb particle errors in preschool children with specific language impairment. *Contemporary Issues in Communication Science & Disorders*, 35:76–83.

Beth Levin. 1993. *English Verb Classes and Alternations: a preliminary investigation*. University of Chicago Press, Chicago, USA.

Barbara Lohse, John A Hawkins, and Thomas Wasow. 2004. Domain minimization in english verb-particle constructions. *Language*, 80(2):238–261.

Catherine Macleod and Ralph Grishman. 1998. COMLEX syntax reference manual, Proteus Project.

B. MacWhinney. 1995. *The CHILDES project: tools for analyzing talk*. Hillsdale, NJ: Lawrence Erlbaum Associates, second edition.

Rosamund E. Moon. 1998. *Fixed Expressions and Idioms in English: A Corpus-based Approach*. Oxford University Press.

Darren Pearce. 2002. A comparative evaluation of collocation extraction techniques. In *Third International Conference on Language Resources and Evaluation (LREC 2002)*, Las Palmas, Canary Islands, Spain. European Language Resources Association.

Carlos Ramisch, Aline Villavicencio, and Christian Boitet. 2010. mwetoolkit: a framework for multiword expression identification. In *Proceedings of the Seventh International Conference on Language Resources and Evaluation (LREC 2010)*, Malta, May. European Language Resources Association.

Ivan Sag, Timothy Baldwin, Francis Bond, Ann Copestake, and Dan Flickinger. 2002. Multiword expressions: A pain in the neck for NLP. In *Proceedings of the 3rd International Conference on Intelligent Text Processing and Computational Linguistics (CICLing-2002)*, volume 2276/2010 of *Lecture Notes in Computer Science*, pages 1–15, Mexico City, Mexico, February. Springer.

K. Sagae, E. Davis, A. Lavie, B. MacWhinney, and S. Wintner. 2010. Morphosyntactic annotation of CHILDES transcripts. *Journal of Child Language*, 37(03):705–729.

J.H. Sawyer. 1999. *Verb adverb and verb particle constructions: their syntax and acquisition*. s.n.

Joan H. Sawyer. 2000. Comments on clayton m. darwin and loretta s. gray's "going after the phrasal verb: An alternative approach to classification". a reader reacts. *TESOL Quarterly*, 34(1):151–159.

Anna Siyanova and Norbert Schmitt. 2007. Native and nonnative use of multi-word vs. one-word verbs. *International Review of Applied Linguistics*, 45:109139.

Anna Siyanova and Norbert Schmitt. 2008. L2 learner production and processing of collocation: A multi-study perspective. *Canadian Modern Language Review*, 64(3):429458.

Aline Villavicencio, Beracah Yankama, Robert Berwick, and Marco Idiart. 2012. A large scale annotated child language construction database. In *Proceedings of the 8th LREC*, Istanbul, Turkey.

Alison Wray. 2002. *Formulaic Language and the Lexicon*. Cambridge University Press, Cambridge, UK.

Alison Wray. 2009. Formulaic language in learners and native speakers. *Language Teaching*, 32(04):213–231.

Phonologic Patterns of Brazilian Portuguese: a grapheme to phoneme converter based study

Vera Vasilévski
Federal University of Santa Catarina, Emerging Linguistic Productivity Lab (LAPLE), Florianopolis, Brazil
sereiad@hotmail.com

Abstract

This paper presents Brazilian Portuguese phoneme patterns of distribution, according to an automatic grammar rules-based grapheme to phoneme converter. The software Nhenhém (Vasilévski, 2008) was used for treating data: written texts which were decoded into phonologic symbols, forming a corpus, and subjected to a statistical analysis. Results support the high level of predictability of Brazilian Portuguese phonemes distribution, the consonant-vowel syllabic pattern as the most common, as well as the stress pattern distribution 'CV.CV#. The efficiency of a phoneme-grapheme converter based entirely on rules is also proven. These results are displayed and discussed, as well as some aspects of Nhe-nhém building.

1 Introduction

The challenging problem of alphabetic systems discovery, i.e., its relationship with the spoken language (Silva Neto, 1988) is the issue discussed, illustrating it with empirical evidence, presenting statistically the Brazilian Portuguese patterns of phoneme distribution, and how they are reflected in the written system. In addition, questions dealing with prosody and syllable are also addressed, with some comments about the spelling agreement that is to be effected in 2013, the goal of which is to standardize the Portuguese spelling in seven countries where it is spoken.

The patterns presented were obtained from the analysis of an automatic grammar rules-based grapheme to phoneme converter designed for dealing with Brazilian Portuguese, the software Nhenhém (Vasilévski, 2008), which is also a syllable parser. The presentation is preceded by a description of the relation between the Portuguese written system and the phonological one and the main problems they cause in finding optimal solutions for writing the program algorithms. Some of the principles of the Portuguese spelling system together with some of the theories that guided the converter construction support the discussion.

2 Spoken and Written Language

Science and also History (Silva Neto, 1988) state that the oral verbal language develops spontaneously whenever traces of humanization are found, whereas the written language is an invention, the intensive and systematic learning of which is necessary in most cases (Scliar-Cabral, 2003a). Linguistic evolution is not just a fact of phonological and phonetic change, however, changes often start as pronunciation modifications (Silva Neto, 1988). Consequently, distinctions fade and disappear, causing homonyms, which must be avoided, so we introduce new words to maintain the independence of signs (Malmberg, 1993). Languages are in perpetual change, although in apparent repose. The distance between the oral and the written system, which is conservative and subject to the literary traditions, becomes increasingly high.

In alphabetic systems, one or more letters (graphemes) represent the phonemes, resulting in units that distinguish meaning in writing (the second articulation), but this representation is not a one-to-one, by virtue of the distance between the oral and the written systems already mentioned. Another divergent principle also occurs: the etymological. Since many spellings are based upon etymological origin (Scliar-Cabral, 2003a) writing does not reproduce the oral system faithfully. Both spoken and written language have their own laws and ways.

2.1 Phonetics and Phonology

While Phonetics is concerned with describing speech sounds (phones) from the point of view of their articulation, perception and physical properties, Phonology studies the phonemes of a language, that is, classes of sounds, abstractly represented in the minds of a linguistic community. In this way phonemic transcription is broad (general), covering all possible phonetic variations of each phoneme. The aim of Phonology is deep invariance, while Phonetics searches surface variations.

There are many schools of Phonology, the most important of which is the Prague Circle, which introduced the functionalist approach, meaning, in this case, that only phonetic differences which cause differences of meaning are relevant. Perception of those differences is a psychic one and implies disregarding any similar phonetic difference which does not provoke a difference meaning. Phonology makes abstraction of the physical properties of sounds, which are the field of Phonetics. Quoting Glossematics, Phonetics studies the expression of sounds (substance of sounds in their multiplicity and variation), and Phonology studies the form (relations, classes, abstract nature, which takes place in the substance) (Malmberg, 1993).

Since the alphabetic principles are based on the phoneme representation, any automatic program must depart from the phonological description of the respective language, which is the case of the Brazilian Portuguese phonological transcription here used.

2.2 Brazilian Portuguese spelling system

Although the rules of registering stress may seem complicated, they facilitate reading. We will present and discuss here only some of the most important rules regarding the spelling system.[1]

Portuguese is a syllable-timed language, i.e., the vast majority of Portuguese words has stressed syllable, leaving aside clictics, which are only a few, but are the most frequently used (prepositions and accusative pronouns). However, the stressed syllable is not signaled for the most frequent stressed words (the ones which receive stress on the penultimate syllable) since Occam's razor principle was adopted, registering only the stress of less frequent stressed words. The criteria for graphically signaling Portuguese words are the following: a) in which syllable stress falls; b) is it a vowel or consonant that ends the word; c) signaling the difference between diphthong and hiatus.

Signaling graphically stress is a powerful hallmark for the reader, because it guides him/her to match the written word with its representation in the mental oral lexicon. Only meta-language is helpful whenever the diacritic is absent for recovering on which syllable stress falls.

The stress diacritics of Portuguese are acute ("chapéu" – hat) and circumflex ("você" – you). A morphosyntactic diacritic is used for signaling the overlap of the preposition "a" with the definite article "a"/"as", or with the demonstrative pronoun "a"/"aquela(s)", "a"/"aquele(s)". For instance, "fui **à** casa da Maria" (I went to Mary's home), "vamos **à**quele lugar" (Let's go to that place).

In Portuguese, stress may relate to the last, penultimate, antepenultimate or, more rarely, to the fourth last syllable of the phonological word, for example, "núpcias" (wedding) → /ˈnu.pʲ .si.aS/ (Câmara Jr., 1986). The phonological word in Portuguese is well defined, and its distinctive mark is stress (Câmara Jr., 1986). The stress position reveals, clearly, the distinctive vowel (Câmara Jr., 1997).

The position of stress does not depend on the phonemic structure of the word. There are no word endings in Portuguese imposing certain stress, but there is a termination which is more frequent, although such frequency is indeterminable phonologically (Câmara Jr., 1997). However, the Portuguese characteristic stress occurs in the penultimate syllable, which gives Portuguese a bass rhythm. Nevertheless, Brazilian Portuguese has more words with stress on the last syllable than European Portuguese, because it incorporated words from the African and Indigenous languages that lived together with the Portuguese colonialists in the past.

Portuguese words main stress is registered graphically according to the pattern frequency in the language. The most frequent word pattern is: ...'C(C)V.C(C)V(s)#, where the last vowel must be "a", "e", "o". These words do not receive any written signal, e.g., "mesa" (table) → /'me.za/,

[1] Portuguese spelling accent system is showed in details and discussed in Vasilévski (2008).

"escreves" (you write) → /eS.'krɛ.viS/, "livro" (book) → /'liv.ru/. Secondly is the pattern ...'C(C)V(s)#, where the last written vowel must be "a", "e", "o". If the last vowel is [-high, -low], it receives a circumflex, e.g., "avô" (grandfather) → /a.'vo/; if the last vowel is [+low], it receives an acute signal, e.g., "sofá" (sofa) → /so.'fa/, "cafés" (coffes) → /ka.'fɛS/, "vovó" (grandma) → /vo.'vɔ/.

On the other hand, the stress of words ending with "i" and "u" – for instance, "abacaxi" (pineapple) and "caju" (cashew) – falls on the last syllable → /a.ba.ka.'ʃi/ and /ka.'ʒu/, unless they have accent mark on another syllable, e.g., "júri" (jury),"bônus" (bonus) → /'ʒu.ri/, /'bo.nuS/.

In Brazil, in most of sociolinguistic varieties, the unstressed final vowels spelled with "e" and "o" neutralize in favor of /i/ and /u/, respectively, when pronounced. This neutralization happens because, if the penultimate or antepenultimate syllable of the word is more intense, the last syllable is reduced: "gente" (people) → /'ʒẽ.ti/, "carro" (car) → /'ka.ʀu/.

Also, stress of words ending in decrescent diphthongs fall on the last syllable: "plebeu" (commoner) → /ple.'bew/, "ramal" (branch) → /ʀa.'maw/, "união" (union) → /u.ni.'ãw/, unless they have accent mark on another syllable: "pônei" (pony) → /'po.nej /. In Portuguese, all words stressed in the antepenultimate syllable are signaled in writing: "número" (number), "cálida" (warm – fem.), "zênite" (zenith) → /'nu.me.ru/, /'ka.li.da/, /'ze.ni.ti/.

Another characteristic that makes the Portuguese system of signaling the stressed syllable in the written system effective comes from the fact that it was guided by phonological intuition. One example is a morphosyntactic diacritic exclusive of certain verbs – "ter" (to have), "vir" (to come), and derivatives – in the third person plural ("têm", "vêm") (Scliar-Cabral, 2003a), thus indicating plural, since third person singular is "tem" and "vem"). The pronunciation, however, does not change: "vem", "vêm" → /vẽj/, /'vẽj/.

In summary, the Portuguese written system of signaling stress is based on the principle of economy (Occam's razor), considering that the most frequent pattern /'CV.CV(s)/ is the one that does not receive a diacritic. Thus, it facilitates decoding, although it may seem more complicated for coding, especially as it is not properly understood by teachers and, therefore, by students. The system has lost some of the qualities based on phonological intuition, due to diachronic changes in the oral system and the lack of spelling rules based on those changes: the 1991 agreement made the situation worse. We will come back to this point.

2.3 The Portuguese syllable

The syllable is the superior unit in which phonemes (vowels and consonants) combine to work on enunciation (Câmara Jr., 1997). Syllable division is deeply studied by Phonology. Its structure types characterize languages. The basic phonemic structure is the syllable, not the phoneme (Jakobson, 1967 apud Câmara Jr., 1986). The syllable in Portuguese can be understood as a set of positions (slope (onset), core (nucleus), and decline (coda)) to be occupied by specific phonemes. The core of the syllable is the only essential position in Portuguese and should be always occupied by a vowel, which is the predominant sound of the syllable. The slope is occupied by consonants and may not be present in the syllable. Further restrictions are made to what may be in decline, which accepts only certain consonants and the semi-vowels /j/, /w/, but can also be empty. In Portuguese the so called free or open syllables, which are the ones that end with a vowel, predominate. This kind of syllables includes simple syllables (V) and open complex (CV). Locked or closed syllables are those ending in consonants (VC, CV(C)C). They are much less frequent in Portuguese, and there are severe constraints, limiting which are the possible consonants in this position (Câmara Jr., 1986).

The most complex syllables in Portuguese are the ones that end with two or three phonemes: CCVVC ("**claus**.tro.fo.bi.a" → /**klawS**.tro.fo.'bi.a/), CCVCC ("**trans**.mu.ta.ção" → /**traNS**.mu.ta.'sawN/ ~ /**trãS**.mu.ta.'sãw/), and CVCCC ("**gangs**.te.ris.mo" → /**gaN.g**ʲ **S**.te.'riS.mu/ ~ /**gã.g**ʲ**S**.te.'riS.mu/). In the last two examples, we can see that there can be two phonological interpretations: the first one considers the existence of nasal consonantal coda and disregards the existence of nasal vowels while the second considers the existence of nasal vowels and the absence of a nasal consonant phoneme in coda position (what the second position admits is the existence of phonetic variants, conditioned by the subsequent consonant). Nhenhém spelling syllable parsing favors the second position. The sequence CCCV is not valid for Brazilian Portuguese. The pronunciation of a foreign word like *stress* is [is.'trɛ.si], so its written form is "es-tresse".

In general, the Portuguese syllable delimitation is clear, but there are three cases where it is floating. There are three groups of vowels contexts in which an unstressed and high vowel may be considered as a semi-vowel, belonging to a diphthong, or as a vowel, forming a hiatus (Câmara Jr., 1997): a) /i/ or /u/ preceded or followed by another unstressed vowel ("var**i**edade", "sa**u**dade", "cu**i**dado"), b) /i / or /u/ followed by a stressed vowel ("p**i**ano", "v**i**ola"), and c) /i/ or /u/ followed by unstressed vowel at the word ending ("índ**ia**", "assíd**uo**"). Phonetically, one can understand these as diphthongs or hiatuses in free variation with no distinctive opposition. Phonologically, however, there is a syllabic not significant variable boundary. In Brazilian Portuguese, they are better understood as hiatus (/va.ri.e.'da.di/, /pi.'ã.nu/, /vi.'ɔ.la/, /'ĩ.di.a/, /a.'si.du.u/), except in the cases in which the second vowel is "i" ou "u", which are better understood as diphthongs: /saw.'da.di/, /kuj.'da.du /.

The above explanation is part of the theory that sustains Nhenhém rules.

3 Methodology, discussion and results

In this section, we present the methodology apllied to the work corpus and the automatic decoder Nhenhém, due to the close relation between them. For the same reason, also we present the results and discuss them.

3.1 The decoder Nhenhém: presentation

The word that gives the program its name, "nhenhém", comes from the Tupi language – spoken by several Indian tribes who lived and continue living in Brazil – and means the endlessly repetition of a movement made by the lips, a sound, as the voice, therefore, an analogue of the word could be "bla, bla, bla".

Nhenhém (/ɲẽ.'ɲẽj/) is a computational program that decodes Brazilian's official writing system into phonological symbols and marks prosody. This program was used for translating, editing, grouping, and searching the work corpus.

What inspired the software development, in 2008, was the high level of transparency of Brazilian Portuguese alphabetic system, although there are some problems, namely the fact the same grapheme "e" or "o" represents respectively two different vowels, /e/, /ɛ/ and /o/, /ɔ/. So, the hypothesis of the availability of the high level of predictability of that system guided the building of a software based on rules, which automatically converted graphemes into phonemes.

Methodologically, the applicative development associates Computational Linguistics, Corpus Linguistics, Statistics, Phonology, and Phonetics. Since the program planning combined proper methodology and linguistic theory, the software could be built in a computer programming language which is not specifically planned for the treatment of human language.

The symbols Nhenhém uses for the conversions are displayed in Tab.1.

Graph	Phon	Example
á	/'ã/	**á**gua (water)
à	/ă/	**à**quela (to which)
â	/'ã/	l**âm**pada (light bulb)
ã	/ã/	maç**ã** (apple)
é	/'ɛ/	p**é** (foot)
é	/'ẽ/	cont**é**m (it contains)
ê	/'e/	l**ê**vedo (barm)
ê	/'ẽ/	t**êm**pora, **ên**fase (temple, emphasis)
e	/ɛ/	**e**ra (era)
e	/i/	elefant**e** (elephant)
í	/'i/	l**í**vido (livid)
í	/' ĩ/	l**í**mpido, **í**ndio (clear, Indian)
i	/j/	pe**i**to (breast)
i	/'j̃/	mu**i**to (much)
	/ʲ/	ad(**i**)vento (advent)
ó	/'ɔ/	p**ó** (powder)
õ	/õ/	an**õ**es (dwarfs)
ô	/'o/	p**ô**s (it put – past)

ô	/'õ/	**côm**puto, **côn**scio (calculation, conscious)
o	/ɔ/	s**o**mente (only)
o	/o/	c**o**mente (you comment)
o	/w/	mã**o** (hand)
o	/u/	pat**o** (duck)
u	/w/	pa**u**, taq**u**ara (wood, bamboo)
ú	/'u/	**ú**til (useful)
ú	/'ũ/	**cúm**plice, an**ún**cio (accomplice, ad)
ü	/w/	cinq**ü**enta (fifty)
c	/s/	**c**ebola (onion)
c	/k/	a**c**udir (to help)
ch	/ʃ/	a**ch**ar (to find)
g	/ʒ/	**g**ente, a**g**ir (people, to act)
gu	/g/	**gu**erra, **gu**itarra (war, guitar)
h		**h**oje, a**h** (today, oh)
j	/ʒ/	**j**anela (window)
l	/w/	anzo**l** (hook)
l	/l/	**l**ençol (sheet)
lh	/ʎ/	ma**lh**a (mesh)
lh	/l/	fi**lh**inho (sonny)
m	/m/	**m**iar (to meow)
n	/n/	a**n**o (year)
nh	/ɲ/	ni**nh**o (nest)
qu	/k/	**qu**ente, ca**qu**i (hot, khaki)
q	/k/	a**q**uático (aquatic)
r	/r/	ce**r**a, p**r**ata (wax, silver)
r	|R|	amo**r** (love)
r	/ʀ/	mel**r**o, en**r**edo (blackbird, plot)
r	/ʀ/	**r**osto (face)
rr	/ʀ/	ama**rr**ar (to tie)
s	/s/	**s**apo (frog)
s	|S|	mo**s**ca, le**s**ma (fly, snail)
ss	/s/	a**ss**ar (to bake)
sc	/s/	fa**sc**inante (fascinating)
sç	/s/	cre**sç**a (it grows up)
s	/z/	a**s**a (wing)
x	/kʲS/	tá**x**i (taxi)
x	|S|	e**x**por (to expose)
x	/z/	e**x**ato (exact)
xc	/s/	e**xc**eção (exception)
z	/z/	a**z**edo (acid)
z	|S|	lu**z** (light)

Table 1: Nhenhém letters, digraphs and corresponding phonemes

3.2 Nhenhém performance

The computational tool we present here is based on rules, i.e., we did not use machine learning based on a training dictionary. Grammatical rules were converted into algorithms and tested within the corpus. A deep and exhaustive study of the grammatical rules that govern the Portuguese written system preceded the design of the tool, consulting the literature on the subject. Internally, the program has all written Portuguese spelling rules (Câmara Jr., 1997, 1986, 1977; Scliar-Cabral, 2003a; Said Ali, 1964; Bechara, 1973; Bisol, 1989; Cagliari, 2002) converted into algorithms, and also the entire Portuguese prosodic system, as it was created by Gonçalves Vianna in 1911, briefly adjusted in 1945 and in 1973 (Bechara, 1973, Scliar-Cabral, 2003a). If the word stress is signaled graphically, the converter reproduces it, if not, Nhenhém applies the spelling rules presented in section 2.2.

Nhenhém bases the translation on a phonologic alphabet, which takes into account the International Phonetic Alphabet (IPA, 2012) fonts, but it gives responses in Arial Unicode MS font (Tab.1). There are no statistics associated to the rules of grammar. We are not worried by the fact that language has many rules: what really matters is that they are general, and that there are rules for the exceptions as well. Unfortunately, some exceptions escape this principle, and became unpredictable, due to the lack of rules. As a result, they are responsible for about 5% or less of Nhenhém translation inaccuracy. We will discuss some of them later.

The software reads relatively huge bunches of data, and bestow phonologic reports with statistical reports. Examining a phonologic corpus rightly assembled, tests done by drawing on the applicative showed that it reaches no less than 98% of accuracy, reproducing the portion of the Brazilian writing system that is predictable by decoding rules. In relation to the written system as a hole, the correctness is not less than

95%. It is known that, to implement the rules in certain groups, it is important to identify the syllabic unit (Almeida & Simões, 2001; Candeias & Perdigão, 2008), however, the first version of Nhenhém (2008) reached at least 95% of accuracy without recognizing the syllabic unit. Such accuracy was measured by testing several texts with the program. This means that, as soon as we approach this issue properly, the results shall become better. Besides this performance, the program also reaches at least 99% of precision at signaling words stress. Such results confirm the hypotheses, and authenticate the high level of predictability of Brazilian alphabetic system, thanks to its phonological basis. It also corroborates that the Brazilian alphabetic system represents the prosody in a logical, accurate, economic and effective manner.

The program does not fulfill some aspects of translating the written texts into phonological transcription, but this happens because there are some exceptions in the Portuguese written system. For instance, in some cases, the letter "x" values are not all predictable by rules. It can be decoded as five different phonemes: /ʃ /, /s/, /z/, /k^{j}S/, /S/. For example: "graxa", "sintaxe", "exame", "nexo", "texto" → /'gra.ʃa/, /sĩ.'ta.si/, /e.'zã.mi/, /'nɛ.k^{j}.su/, /'teS.tu/. The first two examples represent the unpredictable cases.

There are also some cases of ambiguity, for instance, the letter "s" value after "b", e.g.: "observar" (to observe) → /ob^{j}seR'vaR/, "obséquio" (favor) → /ob^{j}'zɛkiu/. So, we consider that "s" as representing an archiphoneme: /ob^{j}Ser 'vaR/ and /ob^{j}'Sɛkiu/ (Vasilévski, 2010).

Morphology can also provoke unpredictable situations. For example, the prefix "trans-", which means "accross", causes a pronunciation ambiguity: "transamazônica" (trans+amazônica) is correctly decoded /trã.za.ma.'zo.ni.ka/, but "transiberiana" (trans+siberiana) is decoded */trã.zi.be.ri.'ã.na/ instead of /trã.si.be.ri.'ã.na/, because there is resyllabification. How to instruct a rules-based program that a rule can either be applied or not for the same situation?

This problem can only be solved by associating morphologycal and phonological rules in the program. We approached this issue deeply in a previous work (Vasilévski, 2008). For now, the solution is to edit the translated text so as to correct all these failures.

Furthermore, the vowels [+low] /ɛ/ and /ɔ/ are written "e" and "o", as mentioned, which makes it hard to predict their values, since /o/ and /e/ have the same coding. When they are stressed

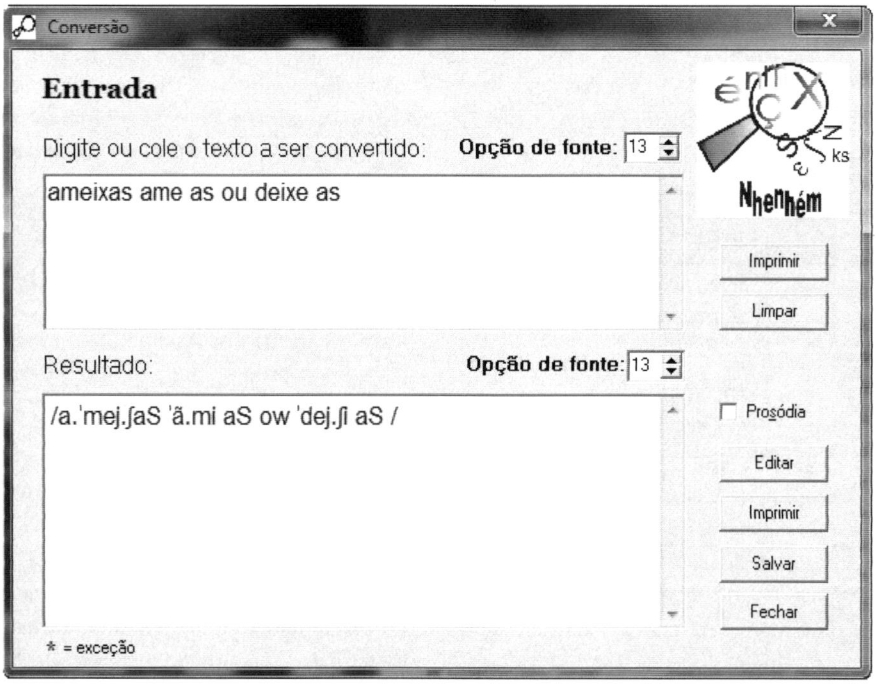

Figure 1: Main screen of the program Nhenhém

and also signaled graphically, the conversion is correct. The reduction of pre-tonic and pos-tonic vowels is also not properly addressed in the Nhenhém algorithm.

Moreover, we decided to consider the so called raising or crescent diphthong as hiatus (Câmara Jr. 1986; Bisol, 1989), therefore words with this ending are decoded as receiving stress on the antepenultimate syllable: "ósseo" → /ˈɔ.si.u/, "história" → /iS.ˈtɔ.ri.a/, "náusea" → /ˈnaw.zi.a/, "ócio" → /ˈɔ.si.u/.

In 2010, Nhenhém was translated into another computer language, and so we could improve its performance. We incremented the main algorithm so that the system became capable of providing the phonological syllabic division, and, consequently, the spelling syllabic division, with at least 99% accuracy. In this way it became easy to signal the stressed syllable, since its 2008 version signaled only the stressed vowel. We used this renewed algorithm to make an automatic syllable parsing for Brazilian Portuguese (Vasilévski, 2010), and we had to solve the problem of syllabication of words that contained hyphen, such as "beija-flor" (hummingbird), "pé-de-moleque" (a peanut candy), "dever-se-ia" (verb to have a duty, conjugated for third person singular, Past Future Indicative, synthetic passive voice, with mesoclisis), and solved them (Vasilévski, 2011).

In addition, we built an interface between Nhenhém and the software Laça-palavras (Vasilévski & Araújo, 2010; Scliar-Cabral & Vasilévski, 2011), which is used for linguistic research. Furthermore, we used the Nhenhém prosodic-phonological algorithm for building a program for speech therapy (Blasi & Vasilévski, 2011), consulting specific literature (Scliar-Cabral, 2003b). This program has been tested and the results were encouraging (Garcez, Blasi, Vasilévski, 2011).

The text is converted while the user types it or pastes it. Pasted texts must have simple formatting, that is, no capital letters. The stressed vowel is signaled by an order from the user. Fig. 1 shows the result for the text "ameixas ame-as ou deixe-as".[2] In the field Resultado (result), the text entry appears converted into phonological symbols. The stressed syllable is signaled by the prosody mark before its first symbol.

The Nhenhém user can automatically convert either one word or a 20 pages text, edit it, save it, research it and print it. As the system conversion is rightly esteemed on at least 95% of accuracy, it allows the user to edit the unsolved 5% (or less) failure rate text, converting, replacing and inserting symbols, adjusting to dialects. The program also allows several texts to be recorded in a database for specific use in statistical reports.

3.3 Phonologic Corpus

In order to test Nhenhém, and also to investigate phonologic patterns of Brazilian written Portuguese, we assembled a corpus with six articles, published in 2007 in a journal of Brazilian dentistry. They are technical and scientific texts, revised, and updated, which were not produced to be used in linguistics research (Sinclair, 1991; Leech, 1992).

The six texts were pre-edited in a text editor, individually, before pasting on Nhe-nhém. Foreign words, words that contained graphemes that do not belong to Portuguese written system and measurement units were eliminated, as well as some acronyms. Some of them could be replaced by its spelling form. The system excludes punctuation, hyphen, quotation marks, and some other symbols by itself, so, they do not need to be treated previously.

In order to reduce chances of conversion errors, care must be taken to ensure the texts' perfect readability by Nhenhém. After this preparation, the corpus texts were pasted on the program, converted, printed, checked, edited, re-checked, and saved for research. The exceptions were searched and edited so as to obtain text correct translations. The texts were loaded for generating statistical reports: the numbers, which will be now exposed, were generated and, as such, are reliable.

3.4 Statistical Report: The Phonologic Patterns

The corpus, after conversion, totalized 69,787 phonemes, being distributed into 33,226 syllabic phonemes (vowels), 3,069 non-syllabic phonemes (semi-vowels), and 33,492 consonant phonemes. Such numbers represent 47.61%, 4.40%, and 47.99% respectively of the total.

To confirm the results, we tested only one of the six texts belonging to the corpus (10,904 phonemes), the numbers of which we present in details (Fig. 2). The main features (traços

[2] Plums love them or leave them – a poem by Paulo Leminski (1991).

principais) distribution is: 47.98% syllabic phonemes, 3.85% non-syllabic phonemes, and 48.17% consonant phonemes. The results are very similar.

Also, the statistical report (Relatório estatístico fonológico) provides phoneme individual distribution, as Tab. 2 displays for the 10,904 phonemes text.

Sistema de conversão grafema-fonema - v.1.0

Relatório estatístico fonológico

TRAÇOS PRINCIPAIS

Silábicos	Assilábicos	Consonantais
5232	420	5252
47,98%	3,85%	48,17%

FONEMAS VOCÁLICOS

Zona de articulação	Timbre	Via de emissão	Movimento dos lábios
Anteriores 2379 42,09%	**Altos** 2503 44,29%	**Orais** 4973 87,99%	**Arredondados** 1713 30,31%
Posteriores 3273 57,91%	**Médios** 1377 24,36%	**Nasais** 679 12,01%	**Distensos** 3939 69,69%
	Baixos 1772 31,35%		

FONEMAS CONSONANTAIS

Modo de articulação			Ponto de articulação	Via de emissão	Fonação
Oclusivos 2725 51,88%			**Anterior** 3339 63,58%	**Orais** 4765 90,73%	**Surdos** 2246 48,95%
Constritivos 2527 48,12%			**Posterior** 877 16,70%	**Nasais** 487 9,27%	**Sonoros** 2342 51,05%
Fricativos 1490 58,96%	**Vibrantes** 784 31,02%	**Laterais** 253 10,01%	**Labial** 1036 19,73%		

FONEMAS ANALISADOS: **10904**

Figure 2: Nhenhém statistical report general distribution

In regard to the vowels (fonemas vocálicos), their distribution is: Tongue position: 42.09% front, 57.91% back; Tongue height: 44.29% high, 24.36% mid, 31.36% low; Airstream way (refers to the route taken by the air flow during vocalization): 87.99% oral, 12.01% nasal; Lip rounding: 30.31% rounded, 69.69% unrounded.

The distribution of consonants is: Manner of articulation: 51.88% occlusive, and 48.12% constrictive, distributed as follows: 58.96% fricative, 31.02% vibrating, 10.01% lateral; Place of articulation: 63.58% front, 16.70% back, 19.73% labial; Airstream way: 90.73% oral, 9.27% nasal (oral and nasal); Phonation: 48.95% unvoiced, 51.05% voiced – the archiphonemes |S| and |R| are not included in these numbers, because they neutralize features.

Ph	%	Q		Ph	%	Q
/a/	12,28	1339		|R|	1,86	203
/i/	11,30	1232		/n/	1,81	197
/u/	6,71	732		/f/	1,33	145
/t/	6,63	723		/j/	1,23	134
/e/	5,39	588		/v/	1,17	128
/ l /	5,11	557		/õ/	1,15	125
/r/	4,44	484		/ɔ/	1,10	120
|S|	4,23	461		/b/	0,94	102
/s/	4,15	453		/ʀ/	0,89	97
/k/	3,99	435		/ɛ/	0,84	92
/o/	3,86	421		/ĩ/	0,80	87

/p/	3,51	383		/ʒ/	0,56	61
/w/	2,60	283		/g/	0,35	38
/m/	2,55	278		/ũ/	0,29	32
/ẽ /	2,23	243		/ʎ/	0,19	21
/d/	2,13	232		/ɲ/	0,11	12
/z/	2,13	232		/ʃ/	0,09	10
/ã/	2,03	221		j̃/	0,03	3

Table 2: Corpus phoneme individual distribution

A journalistic text composed by 8,454 phonemes was prepared and tested individually by Nhenhém, and the results were similar, since the differences were around 1%. So, the results and also the numbers that show the phonologic patterns of Brazilian Portuguese seem reliable. We tried to find another program or even study that approaches this issue in a similar way, that is, a one that determines the segments from their features and inform such statistics, using corpus, but we did not find any. So, for awhile, we could not make comparisons in order to confirm the reliability of the numbers we have presented.

A lot can be discussed about the results, but we will make general comments here. The back or posterior vowels occur around 15% plus than the front or minus posterior vowels. The posterior ones that appear most are /a/ and /u/, and, among the front, /i/, which occurs only 1% less than /a/. So, the vowel that occurs most in Portuguese is /a/, closely followed by /i/.

The semi-vowel / j̃/ occurs only in the word "muito" (many, much) → /'muj̃.tu/ and derived forms. The /ʲ/ is computed with /i/, since the first occurs when in a word there is a sequence of two consonants which ordinarily are not a coda, and belong to different syllable. In this case, the epenthetic /ʲ/ occurs while such sequence is pronounced. So, this inserted phoneme works as core of a phonological syllable: "opção" (option), "cacto" (cactus) → /o.pʲ.'sãw/, /ka.kʲ.tu/.

In relation to the consonant phonemes, there is balance in the occurrence of constrictive and occlusive, although occlusive always occur around 3% more than the constrictive ones.

From the results, we find that Brazilian Portuguese phonemic distribution is uniform, once the amount of vowels and consonants tend to be around 50% each. Furthermore, it is possible to deduce that CV (consonant+vowel) is the most common syllable pattern of Brazilian Portuguese. The semi-vowels reveal the amount of diphthongs (the real ones, that is, falling or decrescent diphthongs), since the semi-vowels only occur in this case.

We believe that a deeper analysis of these numbers can be very useful for Portuguese language research.

3.5 The Spelling Agreement of 1991 (2009)

Some changes are to occur in Brazilian Portuguese spelling, due to a spelling agreement, according to which at least seven of the countries where Portuguese is spoken must use the same spelling, from 2013 on.

The most important change for Brazilian Portuguese is the exclusion of the shudder ("trema"), since recognizing diacrisis becomes unpredictable, e.g., the pronunciation of "u" on digraphs "gü" and "qü". Thus, "agüentar" (to stand) and "eqüino" (horse), until 2013 correctly decoded as /agwẽˈtaR/ and /eˈkwinu/, will be spelled "aguentar" and "equino", generating the translations */agẽˈtaR/ and */eˈkinu/. In Brazil, shudder use is still very common. For these reason, Nhenhém will preserve this resource in its algorithm.

This means that the alphabetic system loses transparency, that is, loses one of the rules that make it predictable; therefore, reading (decoding) is impaired. Other changes interfere less in the automatic translation, but none of them disturbs the prosody system.

4 Conclusion and Outlooks

The experience of building, testing and using Nhenhém has shown the degree of linguistic texts electronic reading and conversion difficulty. The phonemic level is the easiest to systematize, the difficulty is greater for the syllable level, the morphology level comes next and then the syntax, which is more intricate. The complexity of each level may be attenuated by the systematization of previous levels, because one takes advantage of the other systematization. So, converters like Nhenhém are a step for future work on levels that transcend the phoneme, like we did to the syllable.

Some decisions taken in the system building are objectionable to some and noteworthy to others, as are some of theories chosen. However, this was not optional. The choices came from the need imposed by the programming and, within that, objectivity and intelligibility of existing theories, and beliefs and intuition of teachers, students and other language users. The efficiency of Nhenhém confirms the usefulness of the theories adopted.

Now that we have made the automatic syllable parsing, the project follows. We have been working at making the statistical report to look directly to the syllable, and we believe the results will be worthwhile. Some of the next steps are to build a voice synthesizer from Nhenhém, and improve Nhenhém Fonoaud, which is the program for speech therapy. Also, we are working on rules for reducing that 5% (or less) failure rate at the conversion. Since the conversion tool successfully exploits the close correspondence between orthographic representation and pronunciation in Brazilian Portuguese, it can prove to be useful in a range of applications, like in speech therapy.

Acknowledgements

This project is sponsored by CAPES, entity of the Brazilian government for the qualification of human resources, which we thank.

References

Almeida, José João, Simões, Alberto. 2001. Text to speech – A rewriting system approach. Procesamiento del Lenguaje Natural, 27:247-255. http://journal.sepln.org/sepln/ojs/ojs/index.php/pln/article/view/3366/1854

Bechara, Evanildo. 1973. Moderna gramática portuguesa. 19.ed. Cia. Editora Nacional, São Paulo.

Bisol, Leda. 1989. O ditongo da perspectiva da fonologia atual. Revista Delta, 5(2):185-224.

Blasi, Helena, Vasilévski, Vera. 2011. Programa piloto para transcrição fonética automática na clínica fonoaudiológica. Documentos para el XVI Congresso Internacional de la ALFAL, Universidad de Alcalá, Alcalá de Henares/Madri.

Cagliari, Luiz Carlos. 2002. Análise fonológica: introdução à teoria e à prática. Mercado das Letras, Campinas.

Câmara Jr., Joaquim Mattoso. 1997. Problemas de lingüística descritiva. 16.ed. Vozes, Petrópolis.

Câmara Jr. J. M. 1986. Estrutura da língua portuguesa. 16.ed. Vozes, Petrópolis.

Câmara Jr., J. M. 1977. Para o estudo da fonêmica portuguesa. 2.ed. Padrão, Rio de Janeiro.

Candeias, Sara, Perdigão, Fernando. 2008. Conversor de grafemas para fones baseado em regras para português. In L. Costa, D. Santos, N. Cardoso (Eds.). Perspectivas sobre a Linguateca/Actas do encontro Linguateca: 10 anos, 14, 99-104.

Garcez, Tatiane Moraes, Blasi, Helena Ferro, Vasilévski, Vera. 2011. Aplicação do programa piloto para transcrição fonética automática na clínica fonoaudiológica. Anais do 19º. Congresso Brasileiro e 8º. Congresso Internacional de Fonoaudiologia. São Paulo, Brazil. http://www.sbfa.org.br/portal/suplementorsbfa

International Phonetic Alphabet (IPA). 2012. http://www.langsci.ucl.ac.uk/ipa/ipachart.html

Leminski, Paulo. 1991. La vie en close. Brasiliense, São Paulo.

Leech, Geoffrey. 1992. Corpora and theories of linguistics performance. In J. Svartvik (Org.). Directions in corpus linguistics. Mouton de Gruyter, Berlim.

Malmberg, Bertil. 1993. A fonética: teoria e aplicações. Caderno de Estudos Lingüísticos, 25:7-24.

Said Ali, Manoel. 1964. Gramática secundária e Gramática histórica da língua portuguesa. 3.ed. Editora da UnB, Brasília.

Scliar-Cabral, Leonor. 2003a. Princípios do sistema alfabético do português do Brasil. Contexto, São Paulo.

Scliar-Cabral, Leonor. 2003b. Guia prático de alfabetização. Contexto, São Paulo.

Scliar-Cabral, Leonor, Vasilévski, Vera. 2011. Descrição do português com auxílio de programa computacional de interface. Anais da II Jornada de Descrição do Português (JDP), Cuiabá, Brasil.

Silva Neto, Serafim. 1988. História da língua portuguesa. 5a. ed. Presença, Rio de Janeiro.

Sinclair, John. 1991. Corpus, concordance, collocation. Oxford University Press, Oxford.

Vasilévski, Vera, Araújo, Márcio J. 2010-2012. Laça-palavras: sistema eletrônico para descrição do português brasileiro. LAPLE-UFSC, Florianópolis. https://sites.google.com/ site/sisnhenhem/

Vasilévski, Vera. 2011. O hífen na separação silábica automática. Revista do Simpósio de Estudos Lingüísticos e Literários – SELL, 1(3):657-676.

Vasilévski, Vera. 2010. Divisão silábica automática de texto escrito baseada em princípios fonológicos. Anais do III Encontro de Pós-graduação em Letras da UFS (ENPOLE), São Cristóvão, Sergipe, Brasil.

Vasilévski, Vera. 2008. Construção de um programa computacional para suporte à pesquisa em fonologia do português do Brasil. Tese de doutorado, Universidade Federal de Santa Catarina, Florianópolis, Brasil.

Author Index